Trophy Hunter's Wild Game Cookbook

Barry and Judy Barbour

Barry Barbour stands with Susan Poole Barbour,
his 17-year-old granddaughter, when they are sighting
in her 270 Winchester. Susan hunts with her
FFA group on the Runnels-Pierce Ranch near
Bay City. On her first hunt, she killed the largest deer.

Published By
Cookbook Resources, LLC

Trophy Hunter's Wild Game Cookbook

Printed April 2012

ISBN 978-1-931294-75-1

Library of Congress Number: 2005928038

Edited, Designed, Published in the
United States of America
and Manufactured in China by
Cookbook Resources, LLC
541 Doubletree Drive
Highland Village, Texas 75077
Toll free 866-229-2665
www.cookbookresources.com

Bringing Family and Friends to the Table

Barry Barbour
A Lifetime of Hunting

Excerpts from an article by Bob Brister
Outdoor Editor, Houston Chronicle
January 11, 1970

As soon as I got old enough to hunt, I hunted. I am a native Texan, seventh generation, and was raised on the **family ranch, a 14,000-acre working cattle ranch** in Brazoria County, Texas, which is now the San Bernard National Wildlife Refuge for ducks and geese and other small critters.

My uncle, Donald Poole, taught me the basics of gun safety and hunting, which down in that country is mostly ducks and geese, rabbits, coons, quail and dove.

Aunt Muggie cooked the game that I brought in. I also did a lot of fishing on the San Bernard River that is a ranch boundary on the east. The south boundary is the Gulf of Mexico.

I have many happy memories of my experiences as a young teenager, hunting on the ranch and fishing on the river.

I killed my first deer in Rock Island, Texas with my first cousin, Roswell Burke, on his ranch. I decided that I liked hunting and I've been hunting ever since. Then I got with Pat McKissick from El Maton, Texas and he really taught me the fine art of hunting. We hunted in the Texas Hill Country in Fredericksburg, Comfort and Leakey.

When I graduated from high school, Pat McKissick invited me to go out West with his family. We toured seven western states, New Mexico, Colorado, Wyoming, Montana, Idaho, Utah and Nevada and back home to Texas. My life was never quite the same after that. We went to Jackson Hole, Wyoming and saw the largest elk herd in the world and I said "I'm going to come back out here and go hunting!"

There was a sporting goods store in Bay City called Denn Bros. Sporting Goods. It was owned by "Pop", Joe Denn and his three sons, Herman, Sidney and Manuel. Needless to say, I spent a lot of time and money there. At that time, I was doing a lot of hunting in Texas, but I had not hunted out of state yet.

The Denn boys said, "There is another young man we want you to meet, Barry, who likes to hunt as much as you do." I met Don Ross and the odyssey of a lifetime of hunting began.

From Texas to Alaska, we hunted it all! That first year, Don and I hunted together in Rifle, Colorado with Don's friend, Bud Meeks. We had a great hunt and hunted with him again the next year. After that, we hunted out of Rangely, Colorado on the Kirby Ranch with great success.

We hunted at Durango, Colorado with Ron Nubrose, who flew us in by helicopter to a site where we camped at 13,000 feet. Don and I both killed nice 5-point bull elks that year. (In the western states only 1 side of the rack is counted.)

Many other hunting trips all over western Colorado followed. I was in Houston, Texas at **Frolich and Hood Taxidermy when Don Frolich and Carter Hood** said they wanted me to meet an outfitter from Jackson Hole, Wyoming, Keith Stilson, and his number one guide, Charlie Petersen, Jr. Both of their families had homesteaded the valley. This encounter led to many successful hunting adventures with each of them at Keith's camp and later on when Charlie went on his own. Without these two men, I would never have had the opportunity nor the knowledge to have my own outfitting business. I killed a lot of good elk with Charlie and Keith.

I was greatly influenced by Alaska, the Last Frontier. **My first Alaskan hunt was booked with one of the number one outfitters in Alaska, noted big game outfitter and guide, Ray Loesche,** who killed more Boone and Crockett record book animals than just about anybody. I was introduced to him by my friend, taxidermist Carter Hood. I believe **Ray's caribou still holds the world's record.**

Don Ross and I flew to Anchorage, then to Fairbanks where we caught the train to Healey and there we met Ray Loesche. Considered one of the best bush pilots in Alaska, Ray flew us in a Super Cub to a spike camp in the remote area. **I killed a Dall**

sheep and had to walk 25 miles to kill the sheep and 25 miles back, carrying the sheep on my back. I killed a great moose and two caribou, one with a double shovel.

Other hunting trips followed with Ray Loesche on Lake Iliamna where **I killed a record moose and two record caribou, one was the largest killed in Alaska in 1969 and one of the top 100 in the world.**

I met another highly respected Alaskan native, noted pilot, Buddy Woods of Palmer, while hunting at the Nido Ranch in Laredo, Texas with Dan McCarty. Buddy was considered one of the most highly regarded helicopter and fixed-wing bush pilots in all of Alaska. He owned Woods Air of Palmer.

> *I killed a Dall sheep and had to walk 25 miles to kill the sheep and 25 miles back, carrying the sheep on my back.*

While hunting with Buddy, I killed a brown bear and **another record class caribou.** We flew into King Salmon and then Lake Iliamna, on the Alaskan Peninsula, two very remote areas.

While hunting with Charlie Peterson, Jr. in Jackson Hole, I met his nephew, third-generation Jackson Hole native, **Warren Fleming** and his wife, Linda. Even then, as a young man just back from Vietnam, he had hunted and ridden the majestic mountains all his life. A lasting friendship began.

I wanted to own my own outfitting business and Warren said his cousin, Dave Edmiston had a camp for sale. I bought the hunting business and brought Warren in as my partner in **Fleming and Barbour Big Game Outfitters, Jackson Hole, Wyoming.** We had a very successful hunting business for many years.

Warren has since gone on his own and now has Wolverine Creek Outfitters, north of Jackson Hole in a very coveted area for hunting trophy elk and deer.

Throughout these years, I also hunted in **Alaska and Hondo in the Texas Hill Country,** where Steward Savage invited me to be on a lease. We hunted here for 25 years, where my two sons, Donald and Barry Gorden, learned the pleasures of hunting.

During this same time, I also hunted with Dan McCarty of San Antonio on the **Nido Ranch, a 30,000-acre ranch** leased from Arturo Benevides, a Laredo native. The ranch is located 40 miles west of Laredo. Numerous large South Texas white tail deer were bagged while hunting over 25 years.

> *All of Barry Barbour's trophies were prepared by Carter Hood with Frolich and Hood Taxidermy in Houston, Texas. Carter Hood was an approved measurer for Boone and Crockett records.*

During this time **I killed many trophies from all over North America.** Some were **Boone and Crockett, as well as Rowland Ward records.**

Several years ago, I sold my hunting operation in Jackson Hole to Scott Millward, son of longtime Teton County Sheriff Roger Millward, a third-generation native. Scott came with his father when Roger guided for me and when he was five or six years old he said, "One day, Barry, I'm going to buy this hunting business" and he did. His successful operation carries on and is now called **Shoal Creek Outfitters of Jackson Hole.**

I first met Warren and Linda Fleming in 1970, while hunting with outfitter, Charlie Peterson, Warren's uncle. Warren was 20 years old and had just come home from Vietnam after serving three tours of duty.

Warren was guiding for Charlie and we hunted together that year and had a great hunt. Linda was cooking at the camp.

Warren went to work as the ranch manager of Moosehead Ranch, just north of Jackson Hole in Moran, an awesome guest ranch located in the Teton Mountains. While Warren was at Moosehead, I came up and hunted with him in the **wilderness area of Pilgrim Creek, up on the Yellowstone National Park border** for the next three years. The area was very rugged and remote and the hunting was great.

During those three years, Warren and I talked about getting a hunting camp together. In 1974, Warren's cousin, outfitter Dave Edmonston's hunting business came up for sale. **It was located 40 miles south of Jackson Hole down in the Hoback at Shoal Creek.**

At that time, there were only 42 outfitters in the valley. These outfitter permits had been issued by the U.S. Forest Service and most had been in families for generations. There were no new permits issued. The only way you could get a permit was to buy one of the existing permits and there were not very many for sale.

So, I bought Dave Edmiston's hunting business permit and took Warren in as my partner. **Our base camp was located on Shoal Creek so you could drive to it by car. Hunting was strictly on horseback.** It was the thrill of a lifetime and every hunter's dream come true to be an outfitter.

In the meantime, another hunting business adjacent to ours came up for sale, belonging to R. T. Fisk, the **Tin Can Park.** I purchased this campsite also.

> *To get to Tin Can Park, you had to pack and ride in by horseback for two hours. The area was very remote, located at about 11,000 feet and the hunting was superb, an especially coveted area for hunting trophy mule deer.*

To get to Tin Can Park, you had to pack and ride in by horseback for two hours. The area was very remote, located at about 11,000 feet and the hunting was superb, an especially coveted area for hunting trophy mule deer. This, along with the

7

Shoal Creek area, gave us **access to hunting on 165,000 acres of prime elk, mule deer, moose, bear, antelope and bighorn sheep habitat.** Hunting in the beautiful Wyoming mountains was a wonderful experience.

Our hunting success was 98%. Hunters came from all over the United States. Each hunt lasted seven days, beginning in September and ending the first of November. By requirement of the National Forest Service, we had to put the camp up and tear it down each year, leaving the area pristine and as if no human being had ever been there.

Our accommodations consisted of a large custom-made cook tent and six hunters' tents with wooden floors and wood heaters, plus two guides' tents and one tent where we kept all of our saddles and feed. We had great hunting, great food and great hospitality.

Throughout the years as my interest in hunting grew, I began to go out West. I was greatly influenced by the writings of Jack O'Conner of *Outdoor Life* magazine and by my very good friend from Houston, Bob Brister, who wrote for *Field and Stream* magazine and the *Houston Chronicle*. Bob wrote a very fascinating article on my hunt in Alaska in 1969 with Ray Loesche and the **record class game** we killed. The articles by these two men were so perfectly written and informative that they made you yearn for more.

Within these pages, I have written of memorable hunting experiences that I want to share with other avid sportsmen. It was difficult to decide which stories to write about, because each hunt was a thrill from the first to the last. I have also included some hunting "tales" from other friends in the business, some basic hunting information and some "do's and don'ts" for taking care of your coveted harvest.

May you enjoy reading about these experiences and add these tales to those of your own!

Barry Barbour

Table of Contents

Family-Tested Recipes

The recipes in this cookbook are tried-and-true and each is family-tested. My boys, like most kids, liked just a few things when they were growing up, but they loved these recipes. They always wanted to invite friends over when they knew I was cooking a recipe in this cookbook. And that was enough reward for me.

You don't have to use wild game to try these recipes. I don't have wild game all the time either, so I make lots of substitutions using beef, pork, chicken and turkey. Just check out the TIPS after the recipes for suggestions.

Since my boys and Barry love these recipes, I know you will too! Please, help yourself.

Judy Barbour

The Trip of a Lifetime Changed My Life

Judy Barbour

It is no secret that when I first married, I really did not like for Barry to go hunting, but no matter what, he was going anyway.

After I had the boys, I really did not like his leaving. I didn't want to go, because I didn't like hunting. I did not want to leave the boys and I did not think that I liked the mountains, since I was raised on the Texas Gulf Coast. I suppose that I did not like the mountains only because I hadn't been there.

I always pitched a fit when Barry left, and told him to send postcards to me in Las Vegas, knowing all along that I would be home with the boys and I always reminded him that they always got sick while he was gone. **No matter how awful I acted, it never seemed to spoil his trip.**

Barry had hunted in Colorado, Wyoming and Alaska many times when I felt as if the time had finally come when the boys were old enough that I did not feel as if it were an imposition to leave them with my father and mother-in-law, Dr. and Mrs. Barbour.

I was on my way to Alaska! I began packing my bags and was packing my hair dryer and iron when Barry casually mentioned to me that where we were going there probably would not be any electricity. He said that my mouth dropped two feet, but I packed them anyway.

We flew into Anchorage, one of the most beautiful sites in the world, and then to a remote Indian village on Lake Iliamna on the Alaskan Peninsula where Barry hunted with noted Alaskan outfitters, Denny Thompson and Bill Simms. The accommodations and food were great and they did have electricity.

While there, I explored an old abandoned Indian village and had a great time thinking about long ago.

Barry chartered a Cessna 206 to pick us up and take us back to Anchorage since the commuter only came once a week. As we flew over the vast, snow-covered Alaskan frontier, I looked out the window and said to myself, "I'm an adventurer!" and after that experience, my life was never the same again on the Gulf of Mexico in Texas.

I spent another two weeks at the Captain Cook Hotel in Anchorage, while Barry flew down on the Alaskan Peninsula with Buddy Woods. His wife, Chris, came over from Palmer and spent several days with me. We ate a lot of Alaskan King Crab and had a lot of fun and happy times at the hotel pub, "The Whale's Tale". At the "Crow's Nest" restaurant was a gorgeous view of the sunset on the bay. This was the first time ever I had an adventure on my own without Barry and the boys. **My eyes opened to a whole new world and I had the time of my life in Alaska!**

My Personal Hints for Successful Preparation of Wild Game

Barry Barbour

First of all, there is a misconception that all wild game has a "gamey" taste. Quite the contrary. Wild game has a distinct flavor which differentiates it from beef, lamb, pork and other meats. Many factors can affect its quality and flavor. Among these are proper handling of the meat, weather conditions affecting diet of the game, time of year the game is killed and effects of the mating season. **Wild game can well provide some the most delicious and enticing meat you ever prepared.**

While experimenting and tasting, quite frequently I have personally used certain ingredients which enhanced the flavor of wild game dishes. For instance, I have found that the addition of *Worcestershire sauce* complements the wild game meat. In some recipes only a small amount is needed, and in others, a larger amount is helpful. You will also find that I use garlic liberally throughout the recipes. *Black pepper* is a basic ingredient, used more liberally than with comparative beef dishes.

Some additional seasonings with which you might experiment when the recipe calls for beef bouillon are as follows: *beef stock, chilled and defatted*, from last night's prime rib is terrific; always, always save the stock from roasts, steaks, chicken. It is quite nutritious as well as delicious. *Bovril* is a beef extract made in England. It is excellent and may be found in many specialty grocery stores. *Kitchen Bouquet* and *Wyler's Beef Granules* are also very good for this purpose.

Wine is another essential ingredient in many of the recipes. I have found that *sherry* is very compatible with wild game. As a reminder, cook with sherry or other wine that is the quality you would drink. **This secret alone can be a factor in the success of a magnificent dish.** The use of beer in some of the recipes creates a special taste that is unequalled!

Introduction

You will discover that in most instances throughout the book, if a particular recipes calls for elk, you may substitute deer or beef.

I hope that you will find my suggestions helpful. As you experiment and adapt my recipes to your personal taste and to that of your family and guests, you will find a true appreciation of the uniqueness of wild game dishes.

Jerry Whitfield of Bay City, Texas killed this 6-point, 700-pound bull elk at Fleming-Barbour Outfitters at Shoal Creek near Jackson Hole, Wyoming. (In western states elk horns are counted on 1 side only.)

Buffalo meat has less cholesterol and fewer calories than fish or chicken without the skin. It is very high in essential fatty acids and has a very high ratio of Omega-3 and Omega-6 acids.

Preparation Tips for the Wild Game and Seafood Cooks

One of the biggest problems in serving wild game and seafood is the proper preparation in the field and kitchen.

Here are some tips from Judy and me as well as some "do's and don'ts" for the proper preparation of your harvest and for an enjoyable experience from field to table.

Happy hunting!

Venison

Venison is meat from deer, of course, but also from antelope, elk, caribou, moose and reindeer. Of all the big game animals in this country, none is more popular or widely available than the deer. There are many varieties of this species throughout the United States and virtually every state has a legal hunting season for one type or another of this country's most hunted game animal.

One of Barry Barbour's mule deer shot in the Fleming-Barbour hunting range near Shoal Creek.

Because there is more venison in hunters' freezers than any other wild game, you will find an exciting array of recipes for preparing delicious dishes for your family and friends.

Venison Do's and Don'ts

Do's:

1. Bleed and dress animal in the field as soon as possible.

2. Pack or haul animal into camp and chill to prevent spoilage.

3. To prepare meat for freezer, remove all silver skin, fat and bones. (Leaving bones give the meat a strong flavor.)

4. Wash each individual piece of meat, pat dry and wrap meat in heavy-duty foil or double strength freezer paper. (Double fold wrapper in center.) Tape and shut securely with freezer tape.

5. Label type of venison or other meats, cut of meat and date killed.

6. Frozen meats are best used within one or two months. Use within six months for best flavor as meat becomes stronger in flavor and accumulates freezer burn.

Don'ts:

1. Do not transport animal on hood of vehicle. The heat of the engine will accelerate spoilage of animal.

2. Do not store meat in plastic wrapping.

3. Never cook venison in its own fat. The fat is where all the strong flavor is.

4. Do not refrigerate any longer than you would beef.

Small Game

– Rabbits, raccoons, possums, squirrels, armadillos, muskrat

Do's:

1. Clean out all blood under running water.

2. Cut up game to desired size and soak in ice water with a little salt for 24 hours. Soaking takes out a lot of the wild, gamey taste.

3. After 24 hours, pat dry and remove all visible fat and silver skin. Cook fresh or freeze (wrapped in the same manner as venison).

Don'ts:

1. Do not forget to remove scent glands from rabbits, possums and raccoons.

2. Do not cook an animal with a spotted or discolored liver or lungs because of the possibility of disease.

Game Birds

– Quail, dove, woodchuck, ducks, geese, pheasant, wild turkey, grouse, chuckers and partridge.

One of the favorite sports of all hunters, whether for big game, small game or game birds is bird hunting. Its fun, fast, challenging and exciting. After the hunt, the most asked question is, "Now, what am I going to do with all these birds?"

Within these pages you will find many diverse recipes for the exciting preparation of "all those birds". After you have prepared and served your coveted harvest for family and friends, you will probably be wishing you had more of "all those birds".

Do's:

1. When removing feathers from birds, pull feathers in direction of growth.

2. Pluck, draw, clean and cool as soon as possible.

3. Remove craw from all birds and wash birds.

4. Remove all fat, glands and lungs from birds. Wash thoroughly prior to soaking.

5. Soak in ice water, with a little salt, for 24 hours for best flavor.

6. Always cool dressing prior to stuffing any bird. Your dressing consists of the creation you choose to "stuff" your bird. It may be cornbread, boudin, rice or others. Most dressings are southern cornbread. However, I have created Creole jambalaya rice dressings, sausage dressings and oriental rice and fruit ones.

7. Stuff strong-flavored birds with apple, onion and celery while cooking.

8. Wild geese and turkeys should be cooked well done with an internal temperature of 170°. (Check meat thermometer.)

9. For best taste and quality of leftover meats, remove all bones.

10. Freeze small game birds covered completely in water in clean milk cartons or plastic bags. Seal well. Freeze immediately.

11. Freeze larger game birds in same manner as venison.

12. Cook game birds within 60 days of freezing for maximum flavor.

Don'ts:

1. Do not forget to remove oil sac at base of tail on ducks or geese.

2. Never freeze a bird with stuffing in it.

Seafood

Do's:

1. Secret: Never allow your fish to get warm.

2. Gut and gill fish immediately or as soon as possible.

3. Place in ice chest full of ice.

4. Scale fish against the grain or from tail to head.

5. When storing or transporting fish in ice chest, drain regularly.

6. Fillet fish and place in ice water, add 2 tablespoons salt to water. Place in bottom of refrigerator (the coldest part) and chill one to two days.

7. Rinse salt water off. Put in heavy-duty zip lock bag. Place flat, one layer thick. Zip and push out all air.

8. You may also pat fish dry and freeze fillets in water in milk cartons. Seal and cover securely.

9. Whole fish must be wrapped (as venison) after being cleaned.

10. Thaw fish out in refrigerator and never allow fish to get warm.

Don'ts:

1. Do not store fish in refrigerator longer than 2 days. Refrigerated fish should be laying on a bowl of ice in covered dish. All seafood is fragile and spoils easily.

2. Do not fry frozen fish.

3. Do not overcook fish.

4. Do not leave gills on fish if you plan to cook fish with head.

Comparison of Nutritional Values
(100 gm 3.5 ounces)

Species	Polyunsaturated Fat	Saturated Fat	Monosaturated Fat
Beef	8.2	46.3	45.5
Buffalo	11.8	43.2	45
Mule deer	20.2	48	31.8
Whitetail deer	23.9	45.6	30.6
Elk	24.9	48.4	26.6
Antelope	31.6	41.2	27.1
Moose	39.1	36.6	24.3
Caribou	17	46.6	36.4

On a Clear Day in Wyoming You Can See Forever

Judy Barbour

Barry had hunted all over Texas, Colorado, Wyoming and   Alaska when he really wanted to buy a hunting business   for himself.

The boys, Barry and I left Bay City in the fall of 1974 for Jackson Hole, Wyoming. The boys enrolled in school there for three weeks so we could see how it was going to work out. Barry Gorden was in eighth grade. Donald was a sophomore. The transition worked well for them.

The boys, Barry, Warren Fleming and his wife Linda and I made plans to go to Shoal Creek and take a look at Dave Edmiston's hunting camp that was for sale.

I wasn't so sure that I was ready for this lifestyle change, however the boys and Barry were so excited about it that I didn't want to stand in the way.

We packed a picnic lunch and headed down south through the beautiful Hoback Canyon to School Creek. The mountains were massive, rugged and majestic. The Hoback River was clear, cold and beautiful. The Aspen trees were shimmery and golden. What a breathtaking drive!

These valleys are in the hunting range used by Fleming-Barbour Big Game Outfitters in the Hoback River area south of Jackson Hole, Wyoming.

We went many miles through several gates on the way and when we reached the top of the last ridge before entering Barry's area, we stopped and had our wonderful picnic as we absorbed the view. It was magnificent, Palmer Peak, Eagle Peak, so named because it had a stand of trees shaped like a flying eagle, and many other peaks that were unnamed. The panorama was truly spectacular, just like a picture postcard. I knew in my heart that we were making the right decision. We rode on into the beautiful campsite and met with Dave and Kathy and their boys.

"If you really want to know what kind of person someone is, then take them hunting or fishing because it brings out the best or worst in them. You will find out their true character."

The experience of owning a hunting business and the lifestyle changes that occurred in my life changed my life and my perspective of life forever.

We met wonderful people from all over the world, took them hunting and got to know about their lives. Barry always said, "If you really want to know what kind of person someone is, then take them hunting or fishing because it brings out the best or worst in them. You will find out their true character."

Oh, the friends we made in Jackson Hole! Friends that we will treasure forever. Everyone was wonderful to us and treated us like we were natives.

I had just begun to work on obtaining my private pilot's license in Bay City and now had the privilege of learning from mountain flying authority and FAA Examiner, Sparky Imeson, co-owner with his parents, Paul and Jane, at the FBO at the Jackson Hole airport, Imeson Aviation. I went on to get my commercial, multi-engine instrument ratings and have flown all over the Rocky Mountain states and out West.

I began to write cookbooks, started designing and marketing high fashion, Indian-inspired leather designs and became active in the Ladies' Hospital Auxiliary of St. John's Hospital. My whole life changed! My inspirations from the gorgeous area have been numerous and extensive.

Have You Ever Dreamed About Being an Outfitter? Well, Here Are a Few Basics.

Barry Barbour

First, you must find an outfitter who wants to sell out. There are no new permits issued by the U.S. Forest Service in the State of Wyoming.

After you get your permit okayed with the Forest Service, you must be covered with liability insurance and your outfitter and guides must be licensed by the Wyoming Board of Outfitters and Professional Guides.

Next, you have to put together a staff of experienced, professional, licensed guides who have lived and hunted in that country for most of their lives and who are familiar with the

Warren Fleming of Fleming-Barbour Big Game Outfitters, leads a string of horses and pack mules to set up the deer camp just south of Jackson Hole, Wyoming. Mules are used to carry supplies and hunters because they are more sure-footed than horses.

Third-generation Jackson Hole native, Warren Fleming leads
the pack horses and hunters back to the hunting camp. A large
elk already dressed out is tied onto the pack horse behind.

hunting area. A professional camp cook is a must, one familiar with baking at high altitudes and experienced in all aspects of cooking. It's a known fact that if you eat well, you hunt well. If you get back to camp late at night from hunting all day and you are cold and tired and you come into camp to have a great, hot meal waiting for you, it will put you in a great frame of mind and you will sleep well and be ready to go out again first thing in the morning.

You must make sure that you are equipped with the right vehicles for your operation. This is imperative. For hauling horses, you will need a stock truck or a 4-wheel drive, crew cab truck and a large gooseneck trailer. You will also need a large 4-wheel drive SUV, preferably a 3-quarter ton to 1 ton, no smaller for transporting hunters and all their gear, plus hauling supplies. Then you begin to put the camp together (tents, horses, mules, saddles, pack saddles, tack, etc).

First, and most importantly, you have to build your horse corrals. This is the basis for your hunting business. You build two corrals so you can separate your horses (the ones that have been ridden all day from the ones that will be ridden the next day). You also must have a water trough.

Next, you set up your camp. One of the requirements is that the camp site cannot be permanent because it is in the National Forest. It must be put up at the beginning of hunting season and disassembled completely at the end of the season, leaving the area as if no human beings had ever been there.

I purchased custom-made white wall tents, made in Idaho, to my design and specifications. We constructed board floors and framed up the structures for each tent, a large cook tent, 6 hunter's tents (2 hunters per tent), outfitter's tent, guide tent and saddle tent.

Next, you must purchase your horses and mules. Good horses and mules are at a premium. We have had ten of each, half horses and half mules. Mules are better later on in the season as the weather gets worse; they are more sure-footed and a mule will never hurt itself.

You must purchase saddles, pack saddles, horse blankets and all tack. Tack includes items such as bridles, ropes, halters,

The Fleming-Barbour Big Game Outfitters hunting camp was set up every year. Wyoming hunting regulations state that all campsites must be cleared to pristine condition after each hunting season.

Game is hanging on a line at the hunting camp on
Shoal Creek waiting to be transported to Jackson Hole.

head stalls, bits, buckets for water and feed and scabbards and
saddle bags. We have always taken pride in keeping a good
string of horses and mules that will take you safely into the back
country and are a pleasure to ride to and from the hunting area
each day.

After that, you must get your tents equipped. I designed
our cook tent interior, defining the dining area and kitchen area,
but where you can see the cook preparing the foods. That's
just a big part of the entire ambience. Of course, we had the
board floors, butane lanterns, a large dining table with benches
for seating 10 to 12 people. There was a large wood stove for
warmth and for making coffee. Everyone likes to stand around a
wood fire. The cooking area had a large wood stove for cooking
and baking, a butane ice box, 2 screened-in wooden pantries
to keep our non-perishables and dry goods in (bread, candy,
cookies, apples, oranges, cornmeal, flour, sugar, etc.) so small
rodents, such as mice, could not get in. We gathered water from
Shoal Creek and heated it on the stove to wash our dishes.

Kitchen equipment purchases included skillets, baking
pans, stock pots, saucepans, coffee pots, dishes, utensils and
coffee cups.

24

Each hunter's tent was equipped with two cots, foam mattresses, a wood stove, night stand, mirror, wash basin and pitcher.

It is very important to find a good source for purchasing hay for the entire season; sometimes the supply is scarce when it has been an exceptionally dry, hot season for haying. The hay has to be hauled in at the beginning of the season, because later on when it gets extremely snowy and icy, the roads into camp get almost impassable. You also need to purchase enough feed for most of the season. If you get low on feed near the end of the season, you can always purchase additional feed when you go into town at the end of each hunt and haul it in your vehicle.

You must take into consideration the amount of foods to be purchased for each hunt, planning carefully, because you don't get to run to the nearest store on the corner.

For a particular hunting week you will need to purchase enough food for seven days. We always served coffee, milk, fresh fruit juice and sweet rolls in the mornings. A light lunch of nutritious sandwiches were packed for the hunter or were eaten when you come in from the morning hunt. Sometimes, we had a light snack, hot soup or chili to sustain you from the elements before the evening hunt.

Our dinners have always been lavish and elegant with a rustic, outdoorsy ambience. Ours was the most talked about food in all of the hunting camps! (Our chef, Dave Ringelberg, was a graduate of the Culinary Institute of America, Hyde Park, New York.) The table was set with a red-checkered cloth and illuminated by lantern lights. Hunters, as well as non-hunting spouses or other guests, dined on creative hors d'oeuvres, a delicious salad, an entrée of steaks, wild game, prime rib or Cornish hens served with a starch and fresh vegetables followed by a spectacular, creation-of-the-day dessert. All courses were served with appropriate wines.

First Hunting Season

Barry Barbour

That first hunting season for the Fleming & Barbour Big Game Outfitters was in 1975. All licenses were drawn, first come, first serve, meaning that from all over the state of Wyoming the first outfitters in line at the Wyoming Game and Fish Department in Cheyenne got the permits. The drawing was held on February 1st and licenses were issued for the fall hunting season. (It has since changed and the person securing the permit must mail in his application prior to February 1st. The permits are then selected by computer.)

That first year, all of my friends from my hometown of Bay City, Texas, all put in because of my reputation as a hunter and what I had told them about Warren.

On the eve of January 31st, we chartered a twin-engine Cessna 340 to fly us to Cheyenne. It was piloted by mountain flying authority and FAA examiner, Sparky Imeson, third-generation Jackson Hole native and co-owner with his parents, Paul and Jane Imeson, of Imeson Aviation, FBO, Jackson Hole. Sparky, his wife Darlene and three daughters, Paul and Jane and my wife, sons and many others on that trip have since become lifelong friends.

Warren, Linda, Judy and I boarded the plane with Sparky. The weather was terrible, ice on the runway and definitely IFR (instrument flying) conditions and one of the worst winter storms in years.

We boarded the first 340 only to become aware that the alternator was not functioning properly, so we came back and changed planes to another 340.

Sparky said, "I've got to get these people to Cheyenne or they won't have a hunting season."

Warren, who served three tours of duty in the jungles of Vietnam said, "Maybe we shouldn't go!"

We took off again in very deteriorating weather and "Praise the Lord" we made it to Cheyenne.

We were among the very first in line with 42 applications for permits of elk and deer. We received all the permits and our successful hunting business was launched.

In the next years as our reputation was established, we had hunters from everywhere; however, many, many of my lifelong friends continued to hunt with us every year. We met many new friends whose friendships have been treasured throughout the years.

Start Packin':
A Week-Long Hunting Trip

Hunting License
Sleeping bag
Wool shirts and pants
Long underwear
Wool socks
Leather hunting boots
Thermal rubber boots
Blaze orange cap
Down jacket
Lightweight wool jacket
Wool cap
6 game bags

3 pairs gloves
Rain gear
Cap with earmuffs
Hunting knife
Ammunition
Rifle (minimum 30-06)
Flashlight
Binoculars
Camera and film
Compass
Alarm clock
Personal items
and any medications,
if needed

Please pack your gear in any type of duffel bag. If you are hunting in an area where you have to pack in by horseback or mule, please keep your duffel bag contents to no more than 60 pounds or no longer than 36 inches. Most outfitters furnish scabbards and saddlebags.

The Grand Slam of Hunting

Dall Sheep – Alaska
Stone Sheep – Alberta, British Columbia
Bighorn Sheep – Alberta, British Columbia,
Rocky Mountain states
Desert Bighorn Sheep – Mexico

"The Grand Slam" is considered the ultimate in sheep hunting, every hunter's dream! It is very hard to get licenses for the sheep because they are all on a limited draw. To pursue the dream of attaining all four of the North American sheep species is the ultimate in hunting.

First, you must be fortunate enough to draw the individual licenses. They are drawn in very limited numbers and are also expensive. Secondly, you must have exceptional hunting skills, because the sheep's habitat makes for difficult hunting. Thirdly, the sheep are very intelligent, very elusive and very quick to outwit the hunter. It takes much patience and perseverance, as well as stamina and skill to accomplish the "ultimate in hunting".

The desert bighorn sheep population is very limited and it's difficult to get a game tag. They may be found in areas stretching from Baja California to Texas and include Arizona, California, Utah, Texas, Colorado, Nevada and New Mexico.

This Boone and Crockett record-class Alaskan Barren Ground Caribou was the largest caribou killed in Alaska in 1969. The Boone and Crockett score was 421]! and the spread was 60 inches. It was killed by Barry Barbour on the Alaskan Peninsula with Ray Loesche.

This Dall sheep with a 36-inch curl was killed by Barry Barbour in Alaska with Ray Loesche.

This 6 by 6-point bull elk was killed by Barry Barbour on the Black Tail Butte in the Grand Teton Mountains outside Jackson Hole, Wyoming.

Son-of-a-Gun Stew

This is an Old West specialty of the chuck wagon cook.

1 pound deer or elk steak, chopped
½ pound deer or elk liver, chopped
½ pound deer or elk heart, chopped
1 pound marrow gut, chopped
1 (14 ounce) can beef broth
1 pound deer or elk brains, chopped
1 pound sweetbreads, chopped
Salt and pepper

- Stew venison, liver, heart and marrow gut with beef broth until meat is tender. Add brains and sweetbreads and cook another 2 hours over low heat. Season to taste with salt and pepper. The longer it cooks, the better it is. Add beef broth or water if needed.

Accomplishments of the Boone and Crockett Club members include the foundation of the National Forest Service, the National Park Service and the National Wildlife Refuge System, protection of Yellowstone, Glacier and Denali National Parks, the establishment of the Federal Duck Stamp Program and the passage of the Pittman-Robertson and Lacey Acts.

The Pittman-Robertson and Lacey Acts were passed in 1937. It was called the Federal Aid in Wildlife Restoration. Its purpose was to fund the selection, restoration, rehabilitation and improvement of wildlife habitat and wildlife management research.

SOUTH-OF-THE-ROCKIES WILD GAME TACOS

1½ pounds ground deer, elk or moose venison
Salt and pepper
1 medium onion, chopped
2 packages taco seasoning mix
1 (8 ounce) can tomato sauce
½ cup beef broth
12 taco shells
2 tomatoes, chopped
Lettuce, shredded
1½-2 cups grated cheddar cheese

- Season meat with salt and pepper. Brown meat in skillet, add onions and cook until translucent.

- Drain excess fat. Stir in taco seasoning. Add tomato sauce and beef broth. Bring to boil, reduce heat and simmer uncovered 15-20 minutes. Stir occasionally.

- Microwave taco shells wrapped in damp paper towel on HIGH for about 1 minute to heat. Stuff each taco shell with meat, tomatoes, lettuce and cheese.
  Yield: 12 tacos.

The Boone and Crockett world record for typical whitetail deer lists a 27¼-inch inside spread with 8 points on the right and 6 on the left. It was shot by Milo N. Hanson in Biggar, SK in 1993.

SKIERS' SPECIAL STEW

This is quick and easy to prepare after a day on the slopes!

3 to 4 pounds deer or elk, cubed
Flour and oil
1¼ cups burgundy wine
½ teaspoon thyme, marjoram and parsley flakes
1 teaspoon salt
½ teaspoon black pepper
4 to 5 potatoes, quartered
1 onion
2 large carrots

- Preheat pressure cooker to prevent sticking. Flour meat and brown in oil in pressure cooker.

- Add 1½ cups water, wine, thyme, marjoram, parsley flakes, salt, pepper, potatoes, onion and carrots.

- Place cover and regulator on cooker and cook for 25 minutes with regulator rocking. Yield: 4 servings.

Big game animals were disappearing in America in the early years of the 20th century. Buffalo numbered several hundred and whitetail deer and other big game animals were virtually eliminated in states east of the Mississippi River. Wildlife conservation programs were started to keep big game from extinction and were led by the Boone and Crockett Club founded by Teddy Roosevelt.

Barry's Notoriously Famous Barbecue Sauce

2 garlic cloves, chopped
2 yellow onions, quartered
1 cup oil
2 cups vinegar
Salt and pepper
1½ tablespoons Worcestershire sauce
1 lemon
2 canned jalapeno peppers, seeded, chopped
1 tablespoon dry mustard
¼ cup minced fresh parsley
1 cup ketchup
1 (24 can) case beer, divided

- Combine all ingredients except beer in saucepan, including juice of lemon and half the squeezed lemon rind. Add 1 (12 ounce) can beer to saucepan. (You know what to do with the rest of the beer.)

- Place over high heat and bring to a boil, reduce heat and simmer for 30 minutes or until onions are soft.

- Select meat you want to barbecue: elk, deer, wild hog, armadillo, rabbit, beef, pork ribs – whatever suits your fancy! Prepare charcoal grill and cook meat.

- Baste meat frequently with sauce.

Ross Venison Roast

For a really great venison roast, I asked Maxine Ross, Don Ross's wife, to share her recipe. Read some of her husband's hunting stories on page 61.

**1 (4 to 5 pound) venison roast
Salt, black pepper and oil
Garlic cloves
Celery salt
1 onion, chopped**

- Brown roast very lightly in small amount of bacon grease or oil. Add black pepper, several garlic cloves and celery salt and spike meat with slivers of garlic.

- Place in roasting pan and add 3 to 4 cups water. Place onion on top and around roast. Cook 3 to 4 hours, to desired taste.

Tip: *The deer roast is tastier well done than cooked rare. (Meat may be soaked 1 hour or so in salt or soda water to mellow hint of wild taste, if desired.)*

Venison is meat from deer, as well as meat from antelope, elk, caribou, moose and reindeer. Of all the big game animals, none is more popular or more available than deer.

ELK ROAST MILANO

1 (3 pound) elk roast
1½ teaspoons salt
½ teaspoon pepper
3 tablespoons oil
1 (6 ounce) can tomato paste
1 cup chianti wine
1 bouillon cube
2 onions, sliced
5 whole cloves

- Season roast with salt and pepper. Brown in oil in Dutch oven. Add tomato paste, wine, 2 cups water, bouillon cube, onion, cloves and 4 whole cloves garlic and 1 minced clove.

- Cover and simmer until tender, about 1 hour 30 minutes to 2 hours. Serve with your favorite cooked pasta. Yield: 6 to 8 servings

The Boone and Crockett world record for a typical American elk lists an inside spread of 47⅘-inches with 6 points on the right and 7 points on the left. It was shot by Alonzo Winters in White Mountains, Arizona in 1968.

The Boone and Crockett world record for non-typical American elk with 51⅛-inch spread with 9 points on the right and 11 points on the left. It was picked up in Upper Arrow Lake, BC in 1994.

Venison Stew in Mushroom-Wine Sauce

2 pounds boneless elk or deer, cubed
3 onions, sliced
2 tablespoons oil
2 tablespoons flour
Salt and pepper to taste
1 cup red wine, divided
½ cup beef bouillon

- Brown meat in oil. Sprinkle with flour and seasonings. Stir in half the wine and beef bouillon. Add onions. Simmer slowly for 2 to 3 hours or until tender.

- Add more wine while cooking. Add mushrooms during final 30 minutes of cooking. Serve over hot cooked rice. Yield: 4 to 6 servings

Venison Roast in Wine Sauce

1 elk or deer roast
Marinade:
1 tablespoon garlic powder
1 tablespoon black pepper
1 tablespoon onion powder
½ cup vinegar
½ cup Worcestershire sauce
½ cup ketchup
⅓ cup cabernet wine

- Place roast on heavy-duty foil. Fold foil up around edges. (Do not wrap up.) Pour marinade over roast and refrigerate overnight. Roll roast up tightly in foil. Bake at 350° for 4 or 5 hours. Slice and serve.

Tip: *Alternate meat choice: Beef roast*

Boone and Crockett Pan-Fried Venison Backstrap

1 elk or deer backstrap
¼ cup flour
Creole seasonings to taste
½ cup butter or oil

- Slice backstrap thinly. Tenderize with meat mallet on both sides. Combine flour with Creole seasonings. Season meat with flour mixture.

- In iron skillet, melt butter and heat and fry rapidly over high heat, turning once, until brown on both sides. Make gravy from pan juices.

Tip: Alternate meat choice: Beef or calves liver

Tenderloin Rotel

This makes a great appetizer or entree.

4 to 5 pounds elk or deer tenderloin
3 to 4 tablespoons oil
1 (10 ounce) can diced tomatoes and green chilies
Salt and pepper

- Slice tenderloin across grain into slices about ? to ¼-inch thick. Brown meat in skillet with oil until oil cooks into meat. Add tomatoes and juice to skillet. Cook meat until most of juice is gone. Salt and pepper to taste.

RANCH-STYLE ROAST, BARBECUED OVER THE COALS

1-2 tablespoons prepared mustard
½ cup soy sauce
½ cup tomato sauce
Dash Worcestershire sauce and hot sauce
Salt and pepper to taste
4-5 pound venison roast
2 onions, thinly sliced
3-4 carrots, sliced
2 stalks celery with leaves, cut in 3-inch lengths
1 clove garlic, crushed
2 tablespoons butter

- Prepare charcoal pit or campfire coals.

- Combine mustard, soy sauce, tomato sauce, Worcestershire sauce, hot sauce, salt and pepper.

- Heat to blend. Brown roast on all sides over coals. Rub with butter.

- Place roast and vegetables on large sheet of heavy-duty foil. Cover with sauce. Fold foil and seal edges to keep juices in.

- Cook over low coals 1½ to 2 hours. Serves 8

The Alaska-Yukon barren ground caribou is found in the western Arctic region of Alaska. The Northwest Territories of Central Canada are home to the Central Canada barren ground caribou. The largest caribou species in North America is the mountain caribou and may be found in northern Canada.

FLAMING VENISON TENDERLOIN MEDALLIONS

Fit for kings and good hunters!

6 thick-cut elk or deer tenderloins (backstrap)
9 slices bacon
2 cups diced fresh mushrooms
½ cup minced fresh parsley
¼ cup minced onion
1 garlic clove, minced
¼ cup butter
Salt and pepper to taste
Dash Worcestershire sauce and hot sauce
1 teaspoon dijon-style mustard
2 tablespoons red wine
6 large mushroom caps
Brandy

- Wrap each medallion with slice of bacon and secure with wooden picks. Dice remaining bacon and cook until crisp. Drain fat.

- Add mushrooms, parsley, onions, garlic and butter to pan and brown lightly. Add salt, pepper, Worcestershire, hot sauce, mustard and red wine. Keep warm.

- Broil steaks on grill to desired doneness. Place on large platter and top with mushroom mixture. Place 1 mushroom cap, open side up, on each steak. Fill with warm brandy. Ignite and serve flaming for tableside presentation. Yield: 6 servings.

Tip: *Alternate Meat Choice: Beef tenderloin*

HUNTER'S FAVORITE CHARCOAL-BROILED STEAKS

Venison steaks are always best when cooked medium or rare.

4 large "hunter-size" elk or deer steaks
Salt, pepper and garlic salt to taste
Worcestershire sauce

- Season steaks on each side with salt, pepper, garlic salt and Worcestershire sauce. Let stand while grill heats. Grill steaks over hot coals until desired doneness. Yield: 4 servings

Tip: *Alternate meat choice: Beef T-bone, rib eye, sirloin or tenderloin steaks*

OUTFITTERS' CHARCOAL-BROILED STEAKS

1 garlic clove, pressed
½ cup oil
1 cup red wine
⅛ teaspoon crushed black peppercorns
1 bay leaf
Juice 1 lemon
2 deer or elk steaks, cut to size

- Combine all ingredients, except steaks, to make marinade. In shallow pan, place steaks and pour marinade over each. Refrigerate for several hours, turning steaks to coat evenly.

- Remove steaks from marinade, pat dry and broil over charcoal fire or in oven broiler to desired doneness, basting frequently with marinade.

Tip: *Alternate meat choice: Beef steaks*

CAMPFIRE ELK OR DEER

Elk or deer round steak
½ tablespoon butter
1 (1 ounce) package onion soup mix
1 pound sliced mushrooms
1 cup diced green bell pepper
1 (16 ounce) can peeled, chopped tomatoes
Salt and pepper
Dash garlic powder
1 tablespoon salsa
1 tablespoon cornstarch
1 tablespoon Worcestershire sauce

- Spread center of heavy-duty foil with butter. Cut steaks into serving-size portions and arrange on foil.

- Sprinkle with onion soup mix, mushrooms, bell peppers, tomatoes, salt, pepper, garlic and salsa. Mix cornstarch with Worcestershire sauce and 2 tablespoons water. Pour over meat and vegetables.

- Double wrap and seal foil very well. Place on hot bed of coals and cook for 2 hours or place in roasting pan and bake at 350° for 2 hours.

Tip: *Alternate meat choice: Beef round steak*

The Boone and Crockett world record for mountain caribou lists the inside spread of 45⅝ with 23 points on the right and 21 on the left. It was taken by C. Candler Hunt at Prospector Mountain, Yukon Territory in 1998.

THE BOYS' FAVORITE ELK OR DEER

Growing up with wild game meals made our boys experts on meat dishes. This is one of the best in their opinions. Sometimes, I serve this in a chafing dish with cocktail picks at cocktail parties.

> **4 to 6 pounds elk or deer steak**
> **2 tablespoons oil**
> **¼ to ½ cup soy sauce**
> **Black pepper**

- Cut steak into finger-size strips. Brown in heavy skillet in oil and stir to prevent sticking. Add soy sauce and black pepper to taste.

- Cover and simmer about 10 minutes. Excellent served with hot rice. This serves 3 or 4 hungry boys!

This is the easiest way I know to prepare elk or deer and it is by far the boys' favorite. Quite frankly, they prefer it to any beef.

Once when having company, I asked the boys if they would like "teriyaki" elk, as I had named it, and they quickly replied, "yes", and turned to their friend and said, "Harry, you are going to love it!" Now, that's the kind of praise I love.

The Boone and Crockett world record for Alaska-Yukon moose lists the greatest spread at 65⅛-inches with 19 points on the right and 16 on the left. It was shot by John A. Crouse at Fortymile River, Alaska in 1994.

Hot-to-Trot Elk Steaks

This is a very simple sauce to make and it adds excitement to broiled meat.

Deer or elk steaks
⅔ cup soy sauce
⅔ cup sugar
1 teaspoon sherry
1 garlic clove
Dash ground ginger

- Combine sauce ingredients with 2 tablespoons water and bring to a boil. Lower heat and simmer for 5 minutes. Use as a basting sauce to grill steaks.

Tip: *Alternate meat choice: Ground meat patties*

Exotic big game animals are defined as medium to large-size animals that are not native to the area. Texas has developed exotic herds on large ranches. Exotics include gemsbok, ibex, scimitar-horned oryx, waterbuck, addax, Armenian red sheep, axis deer, blackbuck, bongo, eland, fallow deer, Siberian ibex and sika deer. These animals are carefully managed to get record-class trophies. Many animals qualify for the Texas Game Records of the World and Safari Club International record books.

GRINGO STEAK WITH GREEN CHILIES

These are very good rolled up in hot flour tortillas!

1 (4 ounce) can diced green chilies with liquid
1½ cups ketchup
4 tablespoons wine vinegar
1 garlic clove, minced
4 pounds elk, deer or moose steaks
Freshly ground pepper

- Blend chilies, ketchup, wine vinegar, garlic and liquid from green chilies. Cut 1½-inch thick steaks.

- Place steaks in flat glass casserole and cover with chili mixture. Let stand 2 to 3 hours, turning several times, if not completely covered.

- Remove meat from marinade and sprinkle with pepper. Broil over hot coals to desired doneness. Brush with marinade while cooking. To serve, slice thinly and serve with sauce. Yield: 4 servings

Tip: *Alternate meat choice: Beef skirt steak or flank steak*

The Boone and Crockett world record for typical mule deer lists an inside spread of 30⅞-inch with 6 points on the right and 5 points on the left. It was shot by Doug Burris, Jr. in 1972 in Delores County, Colorado and is owned by Cabela's.

SPARKY'S FANCY PAN-GRILLED ELK OR DEER STEAKS

4 thick-cut individual elk or deer steaks
Salt and pepper
1 tablespoon butter
3 tablespoons oil

- Pat steaks dry. Season with salt and pepper. In heavy skillet over medium-high heat, melt butter with oil.

- When hot, sear steaks on each side until cooked to taste. (Rare steaks, 6 minutes; medium steaks, 7 to 8 minutes; well-done steaks not recommended.) Prepare Fancy Burgundy Sauce (below) and spoon over steaks to serve. Yield: 4 servings.

FANCY BURGUNDY SAUCE:

1 pound fresh mushrooms, sliced
6 tablespoons butter
2 garlic cloves, minced
Salt and pepper to taste
2 teaspoons Worcestershire sauce
½ cup burgundy wine
2 cups game or beef stock or broth

- Melt butter in same skillet where steaks cooked. Deglaze browned bits. Add fresh mushrooms, garlic, salt, pepper and Worcestershire sauce and stir to blend. Saute mushrooms.

- Add wine and cook 5 minutes to reduce. Add rich stock and cook 10 minutes longer to reduce to a glaze. Serve hot over steaks.

Tip: *Alternate meat choice: Thick-cut beef steaks*

BEER-SAUCED KEBABS

MARINADE:

½ bottle beaujolais wine
½ cup oil
1 cup vinegar
¼ cup Worcestershire sauce
2 tablespoons onion salt
1 tablespoon minced garlic
3 tablespoons minced parsley
1 jalapeno pepper, chopped
1 (12 ounce) bottle beer

KEBABS:

3 to 4 pounds elk steak, cubed
3 tomatoes, quartered
1 onion, sliced
1 green pepper, sliced

- Mix all marinade ingredients in bowl and add meat. Marinate for 5 to 6 hours or overnight. Reserve marinade. Thread on skewers, alternate meat and vegetables.

- Grill over coals until cooked to taste. Add 12 ounces beer to reserved marinade and baste frequently. You may broil or cook kebabs in oven. Salt and pepper to taste. Yield: 6 to 8 servings

The Arctic Islands caribou may be found on the islands of the Northwest Territories and Boothia Peninsula.

CODY'S SPECIAL KEBABS

This is a festive dish when served with a fresh fruit cup salad and lime sherbet for dessert. Add a crisp, dry red wine and you have an elegant meal.

⅔ cup dry red wine
¼ cup oil
¼ cup minced fresh parsley
2 onions plus ½ cup grated onion
2 garlic cloves
1 teaspoon salt
1 bay leaf
2 pounds elk or deer, cubed to 1½-inches
2 green bell peppers
3 fresh tomatoes
2 onions, sliced

- Mix wine, oil, parsley, ½ cup grated onion, salt, bay leaf, a little black pepper and garlic cloves. Add meat to marinade.

- Marinate overnight in refrigerator and turn to coat all meat. Drain meat and reserve marinade.

- Clean and quarter bell peppers, tomatoes and onions. Place on skewers, alternating meat cubes and vegetables.

- Cook over open grill or broil in oven and baste with marinade until done.

The moose is the largest member of the deer family. It is found in Alaska, eastern Canada and in the northwestern U.S. Moose is an American Indian word.

Judy Barbour's Famous Southwest-Style Wild Game Swiss Steak

For many years, the only way that I could prepare wild game was in Swiss steak. Forced to learn how to cook lots of game, I went on to experiment and write the highly successful, nationally acclaimed wild game cookbook, Elegant Elk, Delicious Deer.

4 tablespoons flour
Salt, pepper, garlic powder and paprika to taste
2 pounds elk, deer or moose steaks
2 tablespoons oil
1½ (10 ounce) cans tomatoes with green chilies
½ cup chopped celery
½ cup chopped carrots
½ cup chopped onions
½ cup grated cheddar or Monterey Jack cheese

- Mix flour and seasonings, spread on both sides of steaks and tenderize. Reserve any leftover flour mixture. Brown meat in heavy skillet with oil.

- Transfer meat to large shallow baking dish. Blend reserved flour mixture in pan drippings. Add tomatoes with green chilies, celery, carrots and onion. Cook, stirring constantly, until mixture boils. Pour over meat.

- Cover and bake at 350° for 1 hour or until meat is tender. Sprinkle cheese over meat to melt. Yield: 4 servings.

Tip: *Alternate meat choice: Beef round or flank steak*

MUSTARD-GLAZED ELK, DEER OR MOOSE STEAKS

4 slices elk, deer or moose steaks
Prepared mustard
Salt, pepper, garlic powder and paprika
2 tablespoons butter
½ cup beef stock
½ to 1 cup red wine
Fresh parsley, chopped

- Coat steaks with thin layer of mustard. Season with salt, pepper, garlic powder and paprika. Tenderize 1 side of steaks with meat mallet, turn and repeat.

- Brown steaks in heavy skillet in butter. Add beef stock and red wine and simmer 1 hour 30 minutes or until tender. Sprinkle with fresh parsley during last few minutes of cooking. Yield: 4 servings.

Tip: *Alternate meat choice: Beef or veal cutlets*

Large mule deer lose their horns once a year in late winter. As they grow each year they have a "velvet" covering over the horns. As they harden, the deer rub their horns on trees and shrubs to remove the "velvet". The largest set of horns is usually produced when the deer is about 6 years old.

49

WYOMING WAPITI

Wapiti is the Shawnee Indian name for elk.

1 to 2 pounds elk round steak
¼ cup flour
Salt and pepper
3 tablespoons oil
1 cup chopped green onions
½ to 1 cup burgundy wine
2 beef bouillon cubes
1 cup sliced fresh mushrooms
3 cups cooked rice
Tomatoes, parsley for garnish

- Cut meat into 1-inch strips. Coat with flour, salt and pepper. Brown in oil. Add onions and cook 2 to 3 minutes longer.

- Stir in wine, bouillon cubes and mushrooms and bring to a boil. Cover, reduce heat and simmer 2 hours or until tender. Add more wine if necessary. Serve over hot rice.

- Garnish serving platter with fresh tomato wedges and fresh parsley sprigs. Yield: 4 servings.

The American elk or wapiti is classified in the deer family, weighs up to 1000 pounds and stands 5 feet tall at the shoulder.

Dead-Eye Deer Picatta

4 deer steaks, sliced very thin
Flour, salt, pepper, oil
2 tablespoons butter
3 tablespoons lemon juice
2 tablespoons fresh parsley, chopped
1 (8 ounce) package spinach noodles

• Sprinkle steaks with flour, salt and pepper and pound mixture into steaks with edge of saucer.

• Brown steaks quickly in hot oil. Remove to warm platter and cover loosely. Reserve cooking mixture in skillet.

• Prepare noodles according to package directions. Add lemon juice, parsley and butter to skillet. Heat and stir for sauce.

• Arrange meat slices on noodles and top with butter sauce. Garnish with fresh lemon slices and additional parsley sprigs.

Tip: *With a lovely tossed salad and white wine, this is a romantic dinner for two!*

The Boone and Crockett Club was founded in 1887 by Theodore Roosevelt to create an organization of sportsmen and conservationists who would address issues involving wildlife, wildlife habitat and hunting.

ELEGANT ELK BIRDS

8 elk or deer steaks
Salt and pepper
8 thin slices boiled ham
8 thin slices Swiss cheese
2 tablespoons oil
1 garlic clove, minced
12 small white onions, peeled
1 cup chablis wine
4 fresh tomatoes, peeled
1 tablespoon flour
3 tablespoons sherry wine

- Tenderize steaks between sheets of waxed paper until thin. Remove paper. Salt and pepper steaks.

- Roll up each steak with slices of ham and cheese. Secure rolls with toothpicks. In large skillet, brown 8 elk "birds" in oil. Remove birds from oil, add onions and saute in skillet until soft, about 10 minutes.

- Place birds in baking dish. Combine wine and garlic with onions in skillet and pour over birds. Bake at 350° for 35 to 40 minutes with whole tomatoes surrounding birds in baking dish.

- Combine sherry and flour in pan juices and stir until they blend. Pour over birds, onions and tomatoes. Garnish with fresh parsley to serve.

This recipe was first published in Elegant Elk and Delicious Deer *by Judy Barbour.*

Deer Cantonese

1½ pounds deer steak, thinly sliced
2 tablespoons oil
2 cups diagonally sliced celery
2 cups sliced onion
1 (10 ounce) package shredded fresh spinach
1 (14 ounce) can mixed Chinese vegetables
1 teaspoon salt
⅛ teaspoon pepper
¼ cup soy sauce
1 (12 ounce) can beer
1 garlic clove, minced
Hot cooked rice

- Brown meat in oil. Add soy sauce, beer, salt, pepper, garlic and onions. Simmer until tender.

- Add celery, spinach and Chinese vegetables during final 10 to 15 minutes. Do not overcook.

- Make sure vegetables remain crisp. Serve over hot rice. Yield: 4 to 6 servings

Wyoming has more pronghorn antelope than people and is the only state that can make that claim.

ELK ORIENTAL

1 pound (¾-inch thick) elk round steak
¼ cup oil
3 tablespoons soy sauce
1 clove garlic, minced
1 cup diagonally sliced carrots
1 cup diagonally sliced celery
2 cups sliced fresh mushrooms
2 tablespoons cornstarch
Hot cooked rice

- Cut meat into strips. Brown in oil and drain. Add 1 cup water, soy sauce and garlic. Cover and simmer 45 to 55 minutes.

- Add carrots, celery and mushrooms and cook additional 15 to 20 minutes. (Vegetables should be crisp.) Blend ¼ cup cold water and cornstarch in small cup. Add mixture to meat and vegetables to thicken. Serve over hot rice. Yield: 3 or 4 servings

The elk is found mainly in Alaska, southern Canada and the Rocky Mountains, but has lost much of its native habitat. The elk is called red deer in Europe, which is a smaller "cousin". In Europe, moose are called elk; they are also smaller than American moose.

Sweet and Sour Venison Steak

2 pounds deer steak
1 teaspoon salt
¼ teaspoon black pepper
¼ cup flour
2 tablespoons oil
1 cup sugar
¾ cup vinegar
¼ cup soy sauce

- Score and pound steak. Sprinkle with salt and pepper and coat with flour. Heat oil and brown meat. Place in baking pan.

- Combine sugar, vinegar and soy sauce in small saucepan and bring to a boil. Pour sauce over meat and bake uncovered at 350° for 1 hour.

Teriyaki Elk

½ cup chopped onion
2 tablespoons sugar
½ teaspoon ground ginger
1 garlic clove, minced
2 tablespoons peanut oil
½ cup soy sauce
¼ cup sherry wine
2 pounds boneless elk, cut into strips

- Combine onion, sugar, ginger, garlic, oil, soy sauce and sherry and stir well. Mix in meat strips and coat thoroughly. Cover and refrigerate several hours or overnight.

- Thread strips of elk on metal skewers and broil 3 inches from heat, 2 to 3 minutes on each side. Yield: 4 servings

CANTONESE ELK WITH SNOW PEAS

1 pound elk steak, sliced with grain
1½ teaspoons cornstarch
Peanut oil
2 pounds fresh snow peas
2 tablespoons soy sauce
Salt and pepper

- Mix elk meat, cornstarch and 2 teaspoons peanut oil. Stir-fry meat in oil in wok over high heat until it loses its red color. Set meat aside.

- Heat 2 tablespoons oil and stir-fry snow peas for 1 minute until they turn brilliant green. Do not overcook! Return meat to wok, season with additional soy sauce, salt and pepper. Serve with rice. Yield: 4 to 6 servings

ROCKY MOUNTAIN BURGUNDY RAGOUT

2 pounds elk or deer steak
2 tablespoons oil
1 teaspoon thyme
1 bay leaf
1 garlic clove, minced
1 (8 ounce) can tomato sauce
1 cup burgundy wine
1 package fresh mushrooms, sliced
1 cup sliced carrots
Salt and pepper

- Cube meat and brown in oil in heavy skillet. Add thyme, bay leaf, garlic, tomato sauce and burgundy. Cover and simmer 2 hours 30 minutes. Add mushrooms and carrots and simmer until tender, about 30 minutes. Salt and pepper to taste. Yield: 6 servings

DUDE RANCH ELK CHOUFLEUR

1 pound (½-inch thick) boneless round elk or deer
2 tablespoons oil
¼ cup soy sauce
1 small head cauliflower
1 green pepper, cut in strips
1 cup sliced green onions
1 clove garlic, minced
2 tablespoons cornstarch
½ teaspoon sugar
1½ cups beef broth
Hot cooked rice

- Cube meat and brown in oil. Add soy sauce, cook until tender and add water if necessary. Separate cauliflower into flowerets. Add cauliflower, green pepper, green onion and garlic and simmer until vegetables are tender, about 10 minutes.

- Blend cornstarch, sugar and broth. Add to meat mixture. Cook, stirring constantly, to heat and thicken. Serve over hot rice. Yield: 4 to 6 servings

The white-tail deer is found all over North America.
They are fast, alert and big bucks are hard to find.

RUSSIAN STROGANOFF

1 pound elk or deer steak, cut into thin strips
4 tablespoons flour, divided
½ teaspoon salt
4 tablespoons butter, divided
½ pound fresh mushrooms
½ cup chopped onion
1 garlic clove, minced
2 tablespoons butter
1 tablespoon tomato paste
1 (10 ounce) can beef broth or 1 bouillon cube
1 cup sour cream
¼ cup dry white wine
Hot buttered noodles

- Coat meat with 1 tablespoon flour and salt. Brown meat quickly in 2 tablespoons butter. Add mushrooms, onion and garlic. Cook until tender about 3 to 4 minutes. Remove meat and mushrooms.

- Add remaining butter to pan drippings and blend in 3 tablespoons flour. Add tomato paste and stir in beef broth. Cook over medium heat, and stir until sauce is thick and bubbly.

- Return meat and mushrooms to skillet and stir-in sour cream and wine. Cook slowly. Do not boil. Serve over hot buttered noodles. Yield: 4 servings

Large mule deer can weigh as much as 350 pounds.

ROULADEN

3 pounds elk or deer round steak, sliced to ¼-inch thickness
2 onions, finely chopped
1½ pounds chopped fresh mushrooms, divided
½ cup (1 stick) butter, divided
¾ pound thinly sliced cooked ham
1 cup dry red wine
1 cup beef bouillon
1 teaspoon salt
Freshly ground black pepper
2 tablespoons cornstarch
4 tablespoons snipped fresh parsley

- Remove all fat from meat. Tenderize meat with wooden mallet and cut into rectangles. Saute onions and half of mushrooms in 4 tablespoons butter.

- Place slice of ham on each meat slice and fill with onion and mushroom stuffing. Roll up jellyroll fashion and secure with round toothpicks.

- In heavy skillet, melt remaining butter and brown meat rolls. Pour in wine, bouillon and season with salt and pepper. Cover and simmer about 15 minutes, then place meat rolls into casserole.

- Bring juices to boil and add cornstarch and 2 tablespoons water until thick. Add remaining mushrooms. Pour this sauce over meat rolls and bake at 375° for 40 minutes or until tender. Sprinkle with parsley.

Tip: *Serve with red cabbage and dumplings or boiled potatoes and a dry Rhine wine.*

59

CHICKEN-FRIED BACKSTRAP WITH CREAM GRAVY

2 pounds backstrap, sliced ¼-inch thick
1 cup flour
Salt and pepper
2 eggs, slightly beaten
½ cup milk
Oil

CREAM GRAVY:

6 tablespoons bacon or pan drippings
6 tablespoons flour
3 cups hot milk
Salt and pepper

- Combine flour, salt and pepper and dredge steaks in flour mixture to coat well. Combine eggs and milk. Dip steaks in egg mixture and dredge again in flour.

- Heat oil in heavy skillet. Place steaks in hot oil and fry until golden brown on each side. Drain and keep warm.

- Use 6 tablespoons pan drippings from skillet. Add flour, cook and stir mixture until flour browns. Add hot milk and stir to thicken.

- Season with salt and pepper to taste. Pour over warm steaks or serve from gravy bowl.

...And This Is the Truth

Don Ross

Manual Denn introduced Barry and me in 1958. We got to be friends and in 1958 we decided that we would go to Colorado deer hunting. I had a friend named Bud Meeks in Rifle, Colorado. We drove up and we hunted with Bud on West Divide Creek.

We also went to Colorado in 1960 and went to two or three different areas and went on a creek north of Rifle, Colorado called Piceance Creek. That is where we really ran into the most deer we had ever seen in Colorado. We had lots of fun and we've told lots of good stories about those hunts. All of them true, by the way.

One that comes to mind is about the coffee that we were drinking. We were so busy hunting that we didn't have a lot of time for cooking. We would just boil up a big pot of coffee and we drank it until it nearly turned green and got a skim on top of it. Barry's daddy, who was a doctor, told us that we were going to get poisoned off of that coffee, but we never did get killed off, so we kept drinking it.

> *We were hunting big bucks, not just bucks.*

In 1961, we went to a ranch in western Colorado by the name of Kirby Ranch. We developed a good friendship with some people and they had a great hunting area. We were hunting deer because there were no elk in that area at that time. **We were hunting big bucks, not just bucks.** We went to the Kirby Ranch in 1961 and 1962. We both killed some 30-inch mule deer and that's a pretty good mule deer.

In 1963, we hunted on Piceance Creek and we also went over and hunted on Texas Mountain very near Kirby Ranch. Barry killed a buck that was a stag with velvet on his horns. He was a nice, big deer with a big head of horns. It was very unusual to come home with a deer that was still in velvet.

In 1964 we decided that we had killed enough big deer, so we wanted to go elk hunting. I drove up to Colorado and delivered a brahma bull to a man at Montrose, Colorado. On that trip I contacted Ron Nubrose. He ran a helicopter service. He told me to come home and get four or five of my buddies and come back to Colorado when elk season opened. He would take all of our gear up into the mountains and we could stay up there and hunt for a week and then

Don Ross, lifelong friend of Barry Barbour, killed this 5-point, 700-pound bull elk (bottom) and this 8-point, 225-pound mule deer (top) at the Fleming-Barbour Outfitters hunting range at Shoal Creek near Jackson Hole, Wyoming.

he would come and get us and our game out of the mountains. **He dropped us off at 13,000 feet elevation and came to check on us every few days, weather permitting.** The first day of season I killed a five-point bull and a couple of days later Barry killed a nice, five-point bull. We both had a good hunt on our first elk hunt. (In the western states, only one side of elk horns is counted.)

When I was a kid going to school (6 or 7 years old), in my home state of Oklahoma, there was a man who, hunted coyotes out of an airplane.

In 1965, we went to Jackson Hole, Wyoming. We went with an outfitter named Charlie Peterson. There was another friend, Irving Savage, from Bay City who happened to have a sheep permit and moose permit and hunted with Charlie that year. The three of us killed an elk and Irving also got a moose and a sheep. That turned out to be a good hunt and we went back the next year.

It was along about this time that Barry and I started looking for something to hunt in off-season. **When I was a kid going to school (6 or 7 years old), in my home state of Oklahoma, there was a man who, hunted coyotes out of an airplane.** I always wanted to do that. Barry had an airplane and I had a shotgun so we teamed up together and started coyote and wolf hunting. In this area we found out that we had both. That was really a fun thing because Barry did the flying and I did the shooting. Everything worked out beautiful. We never came close to having an accident. I couldn't even begin to tell you how many coyotes and wolves we killed. There were a few mornings that we killed five or six in an hour. We only hunted 2 hours at the most each time. In a period of several years, I think we did a pretty good job helping the rangers control the coyote and wolf population in Matagorda County.

We killed many record-book heads. They said that it would probably be a long time before hunters would equal a record of killing so many big heads on one hunt.

In 1967, we went to Alaska for our first trip. We hunted Dall sheep. We hunted with Roy Loesche on Moody Creek up between Anchorage and Fairbanks near Mount McKinley. We had a good hunt. There were four of us from Bay City: me, Barry, Mr. Albert Faye and Jack Garrett. We killed game and Barry and I each got a good sheep. Sheep are hard to hunt. Mr. Faye and Mr. Garrett, being older men, just could not get to where the sheep were. I was very lucky because I also killed a grizzly bear. That was the beginning of going to Alaska.

In 1968, we went back to Wyoming with Charlie Peterson and both of us got another elk.

In 1969, we went to the Alaskan peninsula where we hunted with noted big game outfitter, Ray Loesche. **We killed many record-book heads. They said that it would probably be a long time before hunters would equal a record of killing so many big heads on one hunt.** So we swapped back and forth between Wyoming and Alaska.

In 1970, we went back to Wyoming. We both got elk.

In 1971, we went back to Alaska with a man by the name of Buddy Woods and Buddy hunted on the Alaskan peninsula. There was also a friend of ours from San Antonio, big game hunter, Dan McCarty. He was hunting with Dan at the same time that we were. We sure did kill some big caribou and both of us got a brown bear.

When you get a big, brown bear, moose and caribou you get just about everything worth anything out of Alaska. I think Barry and I killed everything out of Alaska but a polar bear. I think that is out of the question. At that time, it was a very complicated matter to get a permit.

We did a lot of goose hunting every year. I had a good place. One year I dug a hole in the ground and put a burlap sack over it and we would get in that hole. **Those geese would walk over to that hole with that sack and Barry and I would reach out there and catch them.** We would catch our limit alive and we would pull them down in that hole. When we would get our limit, we would go to the house.

I can show you a picture to back up all of these stories. Some of these may seem like stories, in a sense, but it is the truth.

Don Ross

Some Treasured Hunting Memories

Barry Barbour

Don Gene Taylor, my lifelong friend from Bay City, an avid sportsman and hunter, came up to Jackson Hole to go hunting with me. We met him at the airport, as we did with all of our hunters that arrived by air. We drove to Shoal Creek talking about friends and catching up on all the news since I had been gone from Bay City.

Avid sportsman-hunter, Don Gene Taylor of Bay City, Texas holds this 10-point, 235-pound mule deer taken at Shoal Creek.

The next day it was a cold September morning and we eagerly looked forward to hunting. I got up at 4:30 a.m. to saddle the horses and got Gene up at 5:30 a.m. He came over to the cook tent where I had a good fire going in the wood stove to take the chill off of the air and we had some hot coffee and a sweet roll.

Gene wanted a big deer. I had seen a nice buck earlier in the week, so we mounted our horses, heading out of camp, in the dark, toward Palmer Peak at 9,000 feet elevation. We rode for an hour and it was just starting to break daylight. We got near the top of Palmer Peak, where there were just scattered trees and I saw three deer up ahead. **I stopped and glassed; all three were bucks, one outstanding with his head behind a tree.**

I quietly whispered for Gene to dismount and shoot the deer. He said that he could not see the deer's head and asked me if he was big enough. I was seeing from a different perspective and knew it was the same big deer that I had seen earlier in the week.

65

I told him to take my word for it and to shoot the deer. Being the expert marksman that he was, he fired one shot and the deer dropped. We walked over, about 100 yards away, to the deer and it was a magnificent trophy, one that Gene Taylor had mounted and proudly displayed in his home in Bay City.

Tommy Toolson's Birthday Celebrations

Tommy Toolson, third-generation Jackson Hole native, considered one of the finest guides and outfitters in Wyoming, was guiding for me when I first got the hunting camp and guided for me for many years.

Tommy is not only a great hunter, but very outgoing and personable and well-liked by all the hunters.

Sometimes during each 7-day hunt, Tommy began his drama of sadly moaning around, explaining to the hunters that today was his birthday and he was sad because he could not spend it with his family.

All of the hunters tried to cheer him up with birthday gifts such as guns, gun cases, thermal underwear, sleeping bags, binoculars, money and more.

This ritual went on for many years. Surely, with that many celebrations, Tommy should be about 115 years old by now!

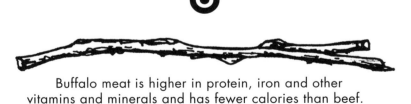

Buffalo meat is higher in protein, iron and other vitamins and minerals and has fewer calories than beef.

Tin Can Park

Barry Barbour

My younger son, Barry Gorden, who was just 14 at the time, a sportswriter from California and Tommy Toolson, a third-generation Jackson Hole native and extraordinary guide, and I met in the cook tent at the hunting camp one morning to plan our hunt for the day. Tommy was guiding the sportswriter who wanted to bag a really big deer since he was there to hunt and write an article about hunting with us. My son was hunting for a big deer too.

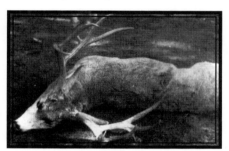

A California sportswriter killed this 12-point mule deer at Fleming-Barbour Outfitters on Shoal Creek near Jackson Hole, Wyoming.

We saddled the horses. Tommy was taking the sportswriter in one direction around the rim of a specific canyon, not far from camp. I was taking Barry Gorden and going around the top side of the canyon. We rode out of camp just a little before daybreak. We hadn't gone far and it was just starting to break day, when I spotted this "big" buck. **His rack wasn't very wide, but was awesomely tall with about 12 points,** 6 on each side. I told Barry Gorden that it was a really good buck and to get off his horse and shoot him.

Barry Gorden then asked me if the deer had a 30-inch spread and I replied, "No, it is about 28 inches, but a really fine buck, heavy, tall and lots of points". He said that he believed he would just wait; he wanted a bigger one. So we rode off and left.

About five minutes later, we heard a shot. Tommy and the sportswriter had come upon the deer and of course the sportswriter killed the deer. Barry Gorden and I turned around and rode back to look at the deer.

Barry Gorden looked at the deer and said, **"Daddy, maybe I should have killed that deer!"** I replied, "Barry Gorden, I told you to kill it".

OUTLAW'S FILET MIGNON

Simple and serves any number deliciously!

Elk or deer ground meat
Bacon slices
Worcestershire sauce
Salt, pepper and garlic powder

- Shape meat into desired number of thick patties. Wrap 1-2 slices bacon around patties and secure with round toothpicks.

- Broil on charcoal grill or in oven broiler. During cooking, sprinkle with Worcestershire sauce and season to taste with salt, pepper and garlic powder.

The meat harvested from big game has no growth hormones, steroids or antibiotics. The animals feed naturally on grasses from the timberline to the valley grasslands. People who cannot eat beef usually have no problem with meat from buffalo or elk.

ELEGANT ELKBURGER

Just think of this as Venison Wellington.

**1 pound ground elk or deer
2 tablespoons prepared mustard
Salt and pepper
Dash garlic salt, hot sauce and Worcestershire sauce
1 (8 ounce) can refrigerated crescent rolls
2 tablespoons dijon-style mustard
2 tablespoons ketchup
1 egg, beaten**

- Mix ground meat and seasonings to taste. Shape into 4 oval burgers about 1-inch thick. Place in small amount of oil in hot skillet and fry until brown all over.

- Unroll crescent dough and separate into 4 rectangles. Press perforations smooth. With a rolling pin, roll each rectangle about 6 x 8 inches in size.

- Place cooked burger on each rectangle and spread with Dijon-style mustard and ketchup. Gently stretch dough up and around burger to cover completely. Seal tightly. Save any excess scraps of dough.

- Turn dough-wrapped burgers over and place on greased cookie sheet. Cut small slits around lower edge for steam vents.

- Cut flowers and leaves from dough scraps. Press on top of burger packages. Brush with beaten egg. Bake at 375° for 15 to 20 minutes or until golden brown. Yield: 4 servings

Tip: *Alternate meat choice: Ground beef*

PISTOL PACKIN' MAMA'S SPECIAL BURGERS

1 (8 ounce) can tomato sauce
1 garlic clove, minced
1 teaspoon Italian spices
1 teaspoon parsley flakes
2 pounds ground elk, deer or moose
Salt and pepper
1 teaspoon Worcestershire sauce
12 slices Italian bread, divided
1 (8 ounce) package grated mozzarella cheese
Spanish olives, sliced

- In small saucepan, combine tomato sauce, garlic, Italian spices and parsley. Simmer 10 to 15 minutes to thicken. Combine meat, salt, pepper and Worcestershire sauce. Shape meat into 6 oval patties. Broil to desired doneness.

- Place meat on 6 bread slices. Spoon sauce over meat, top with cheese and garnish with olive slices.

- Broil until cheese melts. Top with remaining bread slices. Yield: 6 servings

The measuring system adopted by Boone and Crockett in 1950 remains the definitive measuring system used today.

TERIYAKI MEATBALLS

1 pound ground elk or deer
¼ cup chopped onion
¼ cup flour
1 egg
Salt and pepper
¼ cup soy sauce, divided
1 tablespoon oil
3 teaspoons sherry wine
2 tablespoons brown sugar
⅛ teaspoon ground ginger
1 teaspoon garlic salt
2 teaspoons cornstarch

- Combine meat, onion, flour, egg, salt, pepper and 1 tablespoon soy sauce.

- Shape mixture into meatballs. Heat oil and fry meatballs until light brown.

- Combine remaining soy sauce, sherry, ½ cup water, brown sugar, ginger, garlic salt and cornstarch.

- Add meatballs and cook on low heat until sauce thickens. Yield: 4 dozen

By measuring only enduring characters (antlers, horns and skulls) rather than skin length or carcass weight, the measurements may be taken at any given time to verify the measurements and ranking of any animal in its category.

KICK-ASS MEATBALLS

1 pound ground elk or deer
2 tablespoons minced onion
1 egg
¼ cup dry breadcrumbs
Salt and pepper
1 cup beef bouillon
3 tablespoons brown sugar
3 tablespoons soy sauce
¼ cup vinegar
½ cup ketchup

- Mix ground elk or deer with minced onion, slightly beaten egg, breadcrumbs, salt and pepper.

- Blend ingredients well and shape into 1-inch diameter meatballs.

- Heat bouillon until boiling and add meatballs. Simmer covered about 30 minutes.

- Combine brown sugar, soy sauce, vinegar and ketchup. Add to meatballs and simmer about 15 minutes more. Yield: 4 to 6 servings

Big game animals were disappearing in America in the early years of the 20th century. Buffalo numbered several hundred and whitetail deer and other big game animals were virtually eliminated in states east of the Mississippi River. Wildlife conservation programs were started to keep big game from extinction and were led by the Boone and Crockett Club founded by Teddy Roosevelt.

Taos Mountain-Top Meatballs

1 pound ground elk, deer, moose or buffalo
1 cup chopped onion
1 cup chopped green bell pepper
1 cup chopped celery with leaves
2 cups cooked rice
2 eggs, beaten
Salt, pepper and garlic salt
1 (8 ounce) can taco sauce
1 (11 ounce) can condensed cheddar cheese soup

• Combine all ingredients except taco sauce and soup. Mix well and form into 12 meatballs. Place in lightly greased 2½-quart casserole.

• Bake at 350° for 30 minutes, turn and brown evenly. Blend and heat taco sauce and soup.

• Pour over meatballs, cover and continue baking for 30 minutes longer. Yield: 6 servings.

Tip: *Alternate meat choice: Ground beef*

The hunting camp of Fleming-Barbour Outfitters on Shoal Creek outside of Jackson Hole, Wyoming is quiet while hunters are out on the mountains and canyons.

PARTY STROGANOFF MEATBALLS

1 pound ground elk or deer
¼ cup dry breadcrumbs
1 egg, beaten
Salt and pepper
1 garlic clove, minced
2 tablespoons oil
1 cup beef bouillon
1 cup sour cream
¼ cup sherry
1 teaspoon marjoram

- Combine meat, breadcrumbs, egg, salt, pepper and garlic. Shape into balls and brown in oil. Add bouillon, simmer to absorb liquid and turn frequently. Add sour cream, sherry and marjoram.

Tip: *Just adjust quantities to serve a crowd.*

ZUCCHINI-ELK SPAGHETTI

2 tablespoons oil
1 pound ground elk or deer
1 garlic clove, minced
1 pound zucchini, sliced
1 cup sliced green bell pepper
2 tomatoes, peeled, quartered
Salt and pepper
8 ounces spaghetti, cooked, drained

- Heat oil. Add meat and garlic and cook until brown. Add zucchini, green pepper, tomatoes, salt and pepper. Cook over low heat about 30 minutes. Serve meat and vegetable sauce over hot spaghetti. Yield: 4 servings

WYOMING VENISON SPAGHETTI

1½ pounds ground deer or elk
1 teaspoon Worcestershire sauce
2 teaspoons red wine vinegar salad dressing
1 garlic clove, minced
Salt, pepper and oil
1 large onion, chopped
1 green bell pepper, chopped
1 (16 ounce) can tomatoes
1 (10 ounce) can tomatoes with green chilies
1 (6 ounce) can tomato paste
1½ teaspoons Italian seasonings
1 (12 ounce) can whole mushrooms
1 (4 ounce) can ripe olives, sliced
1 cup ketchup
1 (8 ounce) package grated sharp cheddar cheese
1 teaspoon baking soda
Spaghetti
Parmesan cheese

- Mix meat, Worcestershire sauce, red wine vinegar dressing, garlic, salt and pepper. Allow mixture to stand for 1 to 2 hours.

- Saute onion and bell pepper in oil. Add tomatoes, tomato paste, Italian seasonings and oregano. Simmer for 2 hours.

- Brown meat in oil and add to sauce. Cook an additional 30 minutes, stirring occasionally.

- Add mushrooms, olives, ketchup, cheese, a little more salt and pepper. Add baking soda and continue cooking until baking soda stops "fizzing". Cook spaghetti according to package directions. Serve with meat mixture and top with grated parmesan cheese. Serves 6.

Tip: Alternate meat choice: Ground beef

MARVELOUS MANICOTTI

2 (15 ounce) cans tomatoes
2 (8 ounce) cans tomato sauce
2 tablespoons (¼ stick) butter
½ teaspoon garlic salt
8 manicotti shells
1 pound ground deer or elk
¼ cup chopped bell pepper
1 onion, chopped
½ pound mozzarella cheese, grated
Parmesan cheese

- Mix tomatoes, tomato sauce, butter and garlic salt. Cover and simmer 25 minutes. Cook manicotti shells in boiling water about 7 minutes. Drain.

- Brown meat, bell peppers and onion, remove from heat and stir-in mozzarella cheese. Stuff meat mixture into manicotti shells.

- Pour half sauce into baking dish. Place stuffed manicotti on top and cover with remaining sauce.

- Sprinkle with grated parmesan cheese and bake at 375° for 30 minutes. Yield: 4 servings

Buffalo is much leaner than beef and cooks much faster. It is best to cook it rare to medium.

SOUTHWEST MACARONI STAMPEDE

1½ cups uncooked elbow macaroni
1½ pounds ground deer, elk or moose
2 tablespoons dried minced onion
1 (7 ounce) can green chili salsa
2 cups grated sharp cheddar cheese, divided
Salt and pepper
1 (10 ounce) can spicy vegetable juice cocktail
2 large tomatoes, sliced

- Cook macaroni according to package directions and drain. Brown meat until crumbly and drain excess fat, if any.

- Combine macaroni, meat, onion, salsa, 1 cup cheese, salt and pepper. Turn into greased 1½-quart shallow baking dish. Pour vegetable juice over top.

- Place sliced tomatoes on top and sprinkle with remaining cheese. Bake at 350° for 30 to 35 minutes or until bubbly. Let aside 5 minutes prior to serving. Yield: 6 servings

Tip: *Alternate meat choice: Ground beef*

The moose is the largest game animal in North America and can be found primarily in the Rocky Mountains.

CHUCK WAGON CASSEROLE

1 pound ground deer, elk or moose
Salt, pepper, garlic powder, onion powder, oil
½ cup sliced celery with leaves
½ cup sliced green onions with tops
¼ cup chopped red bell pepper
¼ cup chopped green bell pepper
1 package seashell macaroni and cheese dinner
1 (8 ounce) can whole kernel corn, drained
1 (16 ounce) can chopped tomatoes
3 tablespoons tomato paste

- Season meat with dashes of salt, pepper, garlic and onion powder. Shape into meatballs and brown in oil. Add vegetables and cook until tender.

- Prepare macaroni according to package ingredients. Add to meatballs and remaining ingredients. Mix lightly and simmer 15 minutes. Serves 6.

Tip: *Alternate meat choice: Ground beef*

The bowhunting world record Alaskan moose was killed by Dr. Michael L. Cusack at Bear Creek, Alaska in 1973.

BUGSY'S SICILIAN MEAT LOAF

1 pound ground elk or deer
1 garlic clove, minced
½ cup chopped onion
½ cup tomato sauce
¼ cup dry breadcrumbs
Salt and pepper
1 egg, beaten
4 slices cheddar cheese, cut into strips
¼ cup stuffed green olives, sliced
¼ cup ripe olives, sliced

- Mix meat, garlic, onion, tomato sauce, breadcrumbs, salt, pepper and egg. Shape into round patty on baking sheet.

- Bake at 350° for 45 minutes to 1 hour and pour off any excess fat. Arrange cheese and olive slices on top. Return to oven and bake 5 minutes more.
Yield: 4 servings

Mountain goats differ from Dall sheep with longer hair, black horns and deeper chests.

KIDS' SURPRISE FROSTED MEATLOAF

Kids really like this "surprise" meatloaf.

2 pounds ground elk, deer, moose or buffalo
⅔ cup tomato sauce
½ cup dry breadcrumbs
½ cup chopped onion
2 eggs, beaten, divided
1 garlic clove, minced
Salt and pepper
½ teaspoon Italian seasonings
1 teaspoon beef bouillon granules
2 cups hot mashed potatoes
½ cup mayonnaise

- Combine meat, tomato sauce, breadcrumbs, onion, 1 egg, garlic, salt, pepper, Italian seasonings and beef bouillon.

- Shape into oval loaf in shallow baking dish and bake at 350° for 1 hour. Place on ovenproof platter.

- Combine potatoes, remaining egg and salad dressing. "Frost" meatloaf with potato mixture.

- Cook in broiler until light brown. Garnish with parsley. Yield: 8 servings

The pronghorn antelope may be seen in substantial herds in western North America from Canada to Mexico. Herds are in North Dakota, South Dakota, Montana, Wyoming, Nebraska, Utah, Colorado, Kansas, Nevada, California, Texas, New Mexico and Oregon.

Mountain Man's Meat Pie

Your kids will like this with venison or ground beef.

1 pound ground deer or elk
2 (8 ounce) cans tomato sauce, divided
½ cup breadcrumbs
¼ cup chopped onion
¼ cup chopped bell pepper
Salt and pepper
1 garlic clove, minced
1 teaspoon Worcestershire sauce
1 cup rice
1 cup grated cheddar cheese

- Combine meat, half of 1 can tomato sauce, breadcrumbs, onion, bell pepper, salt, pepper, garlic and Worcestershire sauce. Pat mixture into bottom and sides of greased 9-inch pie pan.

- Boil rice in 2 cups water until half-cooked, about 10 minutes. Combine rice, cooking water, 1 can tomato sauce and ¼ cup grated cheese. Place in meat shell. Cover with foil and bake at 350° for 25 minutes.

- Pour off excess juices. Combine remaining half of 1 can tomato sauce and remaining cheese. Bake uncovered 15 minutes longer. Cut into pie shaped wedges to serve. Yield: 4 to 6 servings

The caribou is a wild reindeer and its name is derived from a French-Canadian word. They weigh as much as 700 pounds and stand as tall as 5 feet.

HOBACK RIVER BARBECUED MEAT PIE

1 pound ground deer or elk
¾ cup chopped green onions with tops
¾ cup ketchup
1 tablespoon cider vinegar
1 teaspoon brown sugar
2 tablespoons prepared mustard
Salt and pepper

DUMPLINGS:

1 cup biscuit mix
⅓ cup milk
1 teaspoon parsley flakes

- Brown meat and onions. Add ketchup, vinegar, brown sugar, mustard, salt and pepper. Add a little water if mixture is too thick. Simmer 10 minutes.

- Mix dumpling ingredients. Drop by tablespoonful over top of casserole. Bake at 450° for 12 minutes. Serve hot. Yield: 4 to 6 servings

Tip: Alternate meat choice: Ground beef

Mule deer can be found along the Rocky Mountain regions from Alaska and Canada all the way to Mexico.

West Texas Venison Casserole

1 pound ground deer, elk or moose
1 cup chopped onion
1 garlic clove, minced
Salt and pepper
2 (15 ounce) cans black-eyed peas with jalapenos
2 cups cooked rice
1 (16 ounce) can Mexican-style tomatoes, crushed
1 (8 ounce) package grated cheddar cheese
Paprika

- Brown meat in skillet with onion, garlic, salt and pepper. Combine with black-eyed peas, rice and tomatoes and stir to blend.

- Pour into casserole and cook at 350° for 15 to 20 minutes to heat through. Top with grated cheese and sprinkling of paprika. Return to oven to allow cheese to melt. Yield: 4 to 6 servings

Tip: *Alternate meat choice: Ground beef*

The pronghorn antelope is the fastest animal in North America and can reach speeds of 60-70 mph.

MEXICALI BAKE

This is a quick dish the kids will like.

1½ pounds ground deer or elk
2 tablespoons oil
1 onion, chopped
1 tablespoon flour
1 (4 ounce) can tomato paste
1 teaspoon chili powder
Salt and pepper
1 cup grated cheddar cheese
½ cup sliced ripe olives
1 (18 ounce) package corn muffin mix

- Brown meat in oil and add onion. Stir in flour, tomato paste, chili powder, salt and pepper. Remove from heat.

- Add cheese and olives. Spread evenly over bottom of 9 x 9-inch square baking pan. Prepare muffin mix according to package directions and spread over meat mixture in pan.

- Bake at 400° for 30 to 40 minutes. Let stand for 5 minutes, loosen edges and invert on serving platter. Yield: 8 servings

The National Elk Refuge, in Jackson Hole, Wyoming, holds the only public auction for elk antlers dropped in the preserve. Boy scouts collect the horns for the auction held in May each year.

HUNTERS' DUTCH-OVEN ENCHILADA PIE

2 pounds ground deer, elk or moose
Salt and pepper
1 cup chopped green onions with tops
½ teaspoon prepared mustard
1 (10 ounce) can tomato soup
2 (10 ounce) cans enchilada sauce
9 (8 inch) flour tortillas
2 cups mixed, chopped cheddar and Monterey Jack
cheese

- Over open fire, brown ground meat with salt, pepper and green onions. Add mustard, tomato soup, enchilada sauce and 1 cup water.

- Simmer 5 minutes. Remove ¾ of meat mixture and place in bowl.

- Arrange 2 or 3 tortillas over meat remaining in Dutch oven. Top with layer of cheese. Alternate meat, tortillas and cheese in 3 layers.

- Replace lid on Dutch oven and simmer 10 minutes or until cheese melts and tortillas soften. Yield: 6 to 8 servings

The National Elk Refuge, in Jackson Hole, Wyoming, contains about 10,000 elk that winter outside of Jackson Hole, Wyoming. This is North America's largest protected elk preserve.

GRINGO VENISON ENCHILADAS

1 pound ground venison
¼ cup cooking oil, divided
1 onion, chopped, divided
1 tablespoon chili powder
Salt and pepper
1 (8 ounce) can tomato sauce
1 (10 ounce) can chili without beans
12 (8 inch) corn tortillas
1 (16 ounce) package grated cheddar cheese, divided

- Brown meat in 2 tablespoons oil, ¼ cup chopped onion, chili powder, salt and pepper. Add tomato sauce, 2 cups water and chili. Simmer for 20 minutes.

- Dip tortillas in hot oil and fill each tortilla with 1 teaspoon onion, 2 tablespoons grated cheese and 1 tablespoon chili mixture. Roll up and place seam side down in casserole.

- Top with additional onion, chili mixture and grated cheese. Bake at 350° for 15 minutes. Yield: 4 to 6 servings

Tourists can see large herds of bighorn sheep, deer, elk and bison in the valleys of Wyoming's Absaroka Mountains during the winter around dusk and dawn. Routes leading from Cody, Wyoming along U.S. Highways 14, 16, 20, (Buffalo Bill Cody Scenic Byway), State Highway 296 (Chief Joseph Scenic Highway) and State Highway 291 (South Fork Road) are great viewing areas for large, record-class big game.

CHILI RELLENOS ELK

1 pound ground elk or deer
½ cup chopped onion
2 (4 ounce) cans green chilies, drained
8 ounces shredded cheddar cheese
1½ cups milk
4 eggs, beaten
¼ cup flour
Salt and pepper
½ teaspoon hot pepper sauce

• Brown ground meat and onion. Halve chilies crosswise and remove seeds.

• Place half of chilies in 2-quart baking dish. Sprinkle with salt, pepper and hot pepper sauce. Add half of shredded cheese.

• Top with meat mixture and arrange remaining chilies over meat. Combine remaining ingredients and beat until smooth. Pour over chilies.

• Bake at 350° for 45 minutes. Top with remaining cheese and cook 5 to 10 minutes more. Cool 5 minutes. Yield: 6 servings

Yellowstone was the world's first area to be designated as a National Park. It became Yellowstone National Park in 1872, 18 years before Wyoming became a state.

CHILIES RELLENOS CON CARNE

Great meat-stuffed green chilies

> **1 (10 ounce) can whole green chilies with liquid**
> **⅔ pound ground elk, deer or moose**
> **½ cup raw rice**
> **½ (1 ounce) package taco seasoning mix**
> **1 (8 ounce) can tomato sauce, divided**
> **1 (6 ounce) can vegetable juice**
> **½ cup salsa**
> **1 (6 ounce) roll processed jalapeno cheese, grated**

- Place juice from green chilies in casserole dish. Split chilies and set aside. In bowl, mix ground meat, rice, half of tomato sauce and taco seasoning mix.

- Stuff chilies with meat mixture. Secure each with toothpick.

- Place stuffed chilies in casserole with juices from chilies. Top each with additional tomato sauce.

- Add vegetable juice to pan. Sprinkle peppers salsa on top and around peppers.

- Bake at 350° for 50 to 55 minutes and baste frequently with pan juices. Top each chili with grated cheese and return to oven briefly to barely melt cheese.

- Serve hot and remove toothpicks. Yield: 8 chili rellenos con carne

Tip: *Alternate meat choice: Ground beef*

WORLD'S BEST WILD GAME CHILI

This is Barry Barbour's one-and-only, truly original, doctored, sanctified and anointed chili. He's served up more of this chili to hunters and cowboys than most of us could round up in a lifetime.

2 pounds ground elk, deer, moose or mixed
½ pound ground pork
2 yellow onions, chopped
3 garlic cloves, minced
Oil
1 (16 ounce) can chopped tomatoes
1 (4 ounce) can diced green chilies
4 tablespoons tomato paste
2 pickled jalapeno peppers, seeded, chopped
3 tablespoons chili powder
1 teaspoon cumin
1 teaspoon leaf oregano
2 (14 ounce) cans beef broth
Dash hot sauce
1 (6 pack) beer
Salt and pepper

- Brown meats with onions and garlic in oil in large heavy skillet. Add tomatoes, green chilies, tomato paste, jalapenos, seasonings, beef broth and 5 cups water. Bring mixture to a boil.

- Add 1 beer to pot and drink the rest. Reduce heat to low and cook 4 or 5 hours, stirring occasionally. Adjust seasonings, if necessary. Yield: 3 quarts

WILD BILL'S CHILI CON CARNE

Great on a cold night!

4 pounds ground elk or deer
3 garlic cloves, minced
2 tablespoons oil
4 large bell peppers, slivered
6 large onions, chopped
3 (16 ounce) cans tomatoes
4 (16 ounce) cans kidney beans, drained
2 (6 ounce) cans tomato paste
¼ cup chili powder
2 teaspoons white vinegar
¼ teaspoon red cayenne pepper
3 whole cloves
1 bay leaf
Salt and pepper

- In soup pot, cook garlic in oil until golden. Add meat and brown. Add onions and bell peppers. Add remaining ingredients.

- Cover and cook slowly for 1 hour. If too dry, add additional tomatoes. Serve with rice and crackers. Yield: 8 to 10 servings

Boone and Crockett Club established an official measurement and scoring system for trophy big game in the early 1930's. Revised and adopted in 1950, the measurements and scoring form the current system of scoring big game.

TROPHY CHILI CASSEROLE

1 pound ground deer, elk or moose
1 large onion, chopped
½ cup chopped celery with leaves
1 (15 ounce) can Mexican-style chili beans
Salt and pepper
½ teaspoon chili powder
1 teaspoon minced fresh cilantro
2 cups crushed corn chips
1¼ cups grated cheddar cheese
Sliced ripe olives

- Brown meat in skillet. Add onion and celery and cook until tender. Remove excess fat from skillet, if any. Add beans, salt, pepper, chili powder and cilantro.

- Place layer of chips on bottom of 2-quart casserole. Set aside ½ cup chips and ¼ cup grated cheese for garnish. Alternate layers of remaining chips, cheese and chili.

- Sprinkle center with reserved cheeses and place reserved chips around edge. Top with sliced olives. Bake at 350º for 20 minutes or until heated through. Yield: 6 to 8 servings

Tip: *Alternate meat choice: Ground beef*

The Boone and Crockett Club owns and operates the National Collection of Heads and Horns now housed at the Buffalo Bill Historical Center in Cody, Wyoming.

Eagles' Nest Elkburger Pizza

2½ pounds ground elk
½ cup breadcrumbs
1 onion, chopped
½ cup milk
1 (8 ounce) can tomato sauce
1 garlic clove, minced
1 cup grated romano cheese
Pepperoni slices
Fresh mushrooms, sliced
Mozzarella cheese, shredded

- Combine meat, breadcrumbs, onion, milk and a little salt and pepper. Mix lightly and pat into 14-inch pizza pan.

- Mix tomato sauce and minced garlic. Spread over meat mixture.

- Top with romano cheese. Arrange pepperoni, mushrooms and your favorite ingredients on top. Sprinkle with mozzarella cheese.

- Bake at 450° for 20 to 30 minutes. Cut into wedges. Yield: 6 to 8 servings

Boone and Crockett maintains records for all big game native to North America. This is one of the many ways the organization assesses and improves wildlife management programs.

PILGRIM CREEK STUFFED CABBAGE

⅓ **cup rice**
1 head cabbage
½ **teaspoon salt**
1 egg
1 pound ground elk or deer
½ **onion, finely chopped**
2 (8 ounce) cans tomato sauce, divided
1½ (15 ounce) cans tomatoes
1 bay leaf

- Cook rice according to package directions. Remove 8 outer leaves from head of cabbage. Shred 4 cups cabbage and place in bottom of large baking dish and salt.

- Dip reserved 8 cabbage leaves in boiling water to make them limp. Combine cooked rice, slightly beaten egg, ground deer or elk, onion, salt and pepper and mix well. Add 1 can tomato sauce.

- Divide mixture evenly and fill cabbage leaves. Fold each leaf over and roll, seam side down.

- Secure with round, wooden toothpicks as necessary. Place in baking dish over shredded cabbage.

- Mix canned tomatoes, remaining tomato sauce and bay leaf in saucepan. Simmer 5 minutes and pour over cabbage rolls.

- Cover and bake at 325° for 1 to 1½ hours. Yield: 4 servings

DEER RIBS WITH LUCKY'S BIG-TIME BBQ SOP

3 pounds deer ribs

BARBECUE SOP:

¾ **cup molasses**
¾ **cup ketchup**
1 onion, chopped
2 garlic cloves, minced
Salt and pepper
Hot sauce and Worcestershire sauce
⅓ **cup orange juice**
3 to 4 whole cloves
2 tablespoons oil
2 tablespoons vinegar
1 teaspoon prepared mustard

- Arrange ribs on shallow roasting pan and cover with foil. Bake at 325° for 30 minutes. Pour off excess fat and bake 30 minutes longer.

- Combine all ingredients for barbecue sauce. Bring to boil, reduce heat and simmer 5 minutes. Pour sauce over ribs.

- Bake uncovered at 400°, basting often, for 45 minutes or until tender and brown. Yield: 4 to 6 servings

The Award winners selected by Boone and Crockett receive trophies and the All-Time winners receive trophies and a listing in the Records of North American Big Game.

Horse Fly Oven-Barbecued Wild Game Ribs

5 to 6 pounds wild game ribs (elk, deer, antelope,
   wild hog, sheep)
4 garlic cloves, minced
½ cup lemon juice
½ cup soy sauce
Salt and pepper
¼ cup packed brown sugar
¼ cup distilled vinegar
1 cup ketchup
2 tablespoons Worcestershire sauce
4 to 5 drops hot sauce
2 teaspoons dry mustard
1 tablespoon chopped fresh parsley
1 tablespoon celery seeds
1 tablespoon sweet basil
½ teaspoon chili powder

- Cut ribs individually in serving-size pieces. Place in
  large flat pan. Combine all ingredients for sauce, pour
  sauce over ribs and marinate 2 hours, turning frequently.

- Roast, uncovered at 350° for 1 hour 30 minutes and
  baste occasionally. Cover and continue baking for
  1 hour longer or until tender, basting frequently.
  Yield: 8 servings

Tip: *Alternate meat choice: Beef or pork ribs*

BARBECUED CABRITO OR ANTELOPE

A favorite in Mexico and South Texas, cabrito is the Mexican word for "young kid goat".

1 (25 to 30 pound) whole cabrito or antelope, dressed
Barry's Notoriously Famous Barbecue Sauce (page 33)

- Prepare barbecue pit. Place whole cabrito on pit.
- Baste often with sauce, turning occasionally, so that meat will cook and brown evenly.
- Cook for 6 to 8 hours, depending on size, until well done. Do not undercook, but do not overcook or meat will fall apart. Yield: 10 to 12

The secret to success for cooking cabrito is to baste frequently with sauce to insure tender and juicy meat that is not dry or overly crisp. Serve whole at your next outdoor barbecue or "Fiesta" with all the trimmings.

The Fleming-Barbour Outfitters hunting camp had an area for horses and on the left an area to hang meat. Two sets of horses were used and alternated from one day to another.

Cook's Baked Whole Elk Liver

¼ cup flour
3 pounds elk liver
4 tablespoons bacon drippings
1 onion, sliced
1 cup dry white or red wine
½ cup beef bouillon
1 teaspoon tomato bouillon granules with chicken
    extract
2 tablespoons vinegar
¼ teaspoon whole black peppercorns
2 small bay leaves
½ lemon, thinly sliced

- Combine flour and a little salt and pepper. Sprinkle over liver and coat well.

- Heat bacon drippings in heavy kettle with tight fitting lid. Brown liver well in drippings.

- Add onion, wine, bouillon, bouillon granules and ¼ cup water. Season with remaining ingredients.

- Cover pan and simmer on low for 1 hour or until meat is tender.

- Remove liver to serving platter. Keep hot.

- To make gravy, thicken pan juices with flour or cornstarch. Slice liver and serve with gravy. Yield: 8 to 10 servings

Tip: *Alternate meat choice: Beef liver*

BOONE'S FRYING PAN LIVER

This turns out to be a premium select dish with the mushroom-wine sauce.

3 tablespoons butter
1 pound elk or deer liver, thinly sliced
2 sprigs fresh parsley, chopped
1 (4 ounce) can sliced mushrooms with liquid
1 lemon
¼ cup white or red wine

- Melt butter in frying pan over medium heat and brown liver well on each side. Lower temperature.

- Sprinkle parsley over top of liver and add mushrooms with liquid, juice of lemon and wine.

- Cover, cook slowly (about 10 to 15 minutes) and turn liver occasionally until tender. Add more wine during cooking if necessary to keep moist.

- Add salt and pepper to taste. Serve immediately with pan juices spooned over it. Yield: 4 servings

Tip: *Alternate meat choice: Beef or chicken livers*

In and around the Jackson Hole-Yellowstone area, more than 60 species of mammals and 100 species of birds live.

CROCKETT'S SKILLET LIVER STRIPS

1 pound deer, elk or moose liver, cut in small strips
2 tablespoons (¼ stick) butter
1 teaspoon ketchup
½ teaspoon prepared mustard
½ cup chopped onion

- Saute liver in hot skillet with a little butter until brown. Remove from pan.

- In skillet, add remaining butter, ketchup, mustard and onion and saute. Add liver strips and heat. Serve over hot steamed rice. Yield: 4 servings

Tip: *Alternate meat choice: Beef or chicken livers or duck, turkey or goose livers*

Warren Fleming of Fleming-Barbour Outfitters leads a group of hunters into the hunting range on Shoal Creek outside Jackson Hole, Wyoming. Hunting on the range was accessible only by horseback.

ELK-SAUSAGE WAGON WHEEL PIE

Different and delicious!

1 pound ground elk
½ cup breadcrumbs
1 teaspoon onion powder
1 (9-inch) unbaked pie shell
3 sweet Italian sausages
2 fresh tomatoes
1 cup grated cheddar cheese
12 small green chili peppers

- Combine ground elk, breadcrumbs and onion powder and mix well. Press into unbaked pie shell.

- Remove Italian sausage from casing, mash and spread evenly over meat mixture, leaving ½-inch edge. Bake at 350° for 30 minutes. Remove from oven.

- Peel and slice tomatoes. Halve each slice and arrange around edge of pan. Sprinkle tomatoes with grated cheese.

- Arrange chili peppers spoke-fashion, inside circles of tomatoes. Return to oven and cook 10 minutes more. Serve hot.

The Boone and Crockett Club was the champion for hunting ethics and Fair Chase. "Fair Chase is the ethical, sportsmanlike, and lawful pursuit and taking of free-ranging wild game animals in a manner that does not give the hunter an improper or unfair advantage over the animal. Fair Chase extends beyond the hunt. It is the very core of outdoor ethics, extending to all who enjoy wildlife and wildlands, or who make use of their resources."
www.booneandcrockett.org

Cajun Red Beans and Rice with Wild Game Sausage

Well worth the effort!

1 pound dried red kidney beans
6 cups water
4 tablespoons (½ stick) butter
1½ cups finely chopped green onions with tops
½ cup chopped green bell pepper
½ cup red bell pepper
1 rib celery with leaves, chopped
2 garlic cloves, chopped
Meaty ham bone
1 pound hot smoked, wild game sausage, sliced
Creole seasoning
1 tablespoon sugar
3 to 4 drops hot sauce
Fresh tomato, peeled, chopped
Green onions with tops, sliced

- Wash and sort beans. Drop in pot of boiling water and boil briskly for 2 minutes. Turn off heat and soak beans for 1 hour.

- In heavy casserole or Dutch oven, melt butter and saute vegetables in garlic until soft but not brown. Stir in beans, liquid, ham bone or ham hocks, sausage and seasonings. Bring to a boil, reduce heat and simmer, partially covered, for 3 hours or until beans are tender. (If beans get too dry during cooking, add a little hot water.) Stir frequently.

- Remove ham bone or hocks, cut meat from bones, discard fat and return meat to beans. Serve with hot, fluffy rice and sprinkle with tomatoes, green onions and parsley over the top. Yield: 4 to 6 servings

Tip: *Meat choices: Elk, deer or hot, spicy pork sausage*

VENISON SAUSAGE SKILLET MIX

1 pound bulk venison sausage, crumbled
1 green bell pepper, chopped
2 green onions with tops, chopped
2 celery ribs with leaves, chopped
1 cup raw rice
2 cups boiling chicken broth
1 tablespoon Worcestershire sauce

- Place sausage in skillet and brown. Pour off grease, if any. Add remaining ingredients and stir. Cover and simmer on low heat for 1 hour. Add a little salt and pepper.

Tip: *Alternate meat choice: Pork sausage*

SADDLE-BAGS VENISON JERKY

Great trail food or snack!

3 pounds elk or deer steak
½ cup soy sauce
½ teaspoon salt
¼ teaspoon garlic powder

- Trim fat from meat and cut into long, very thin strips about 2-inches wide. Place in shallow, long dish. Combine remaining ingredients and pour over meat. Marinate 4 hours.

- Preheat oven to 275°. Place meat strips on cooling racks set on baking sheets. Bake for 3 hours or until adequately dried.

Big-Sky Moose Roast

1 moose roast, trimmed
8 to 10 garlic cloves, slivered
Prepared mustard
¼ cup flour
1 to 2 tablespoons beef bouillon granules
Butter or oil
Bacon slices

- Make slits in roast with knife and place garlic slivers in each. Place roast on heavy-duty foil and spread liberally with mustard.

- Sprinkle with flour, a little salt and pepper and beef bouillon granules. Dot with butter or sprinkle with oil.

- Top with several bacon slices. Seal foil tightly. Cook over hot coals until tender.

This 2000-pound Alaskan moose with a 65-inch spread was killed by Barry Barbour on the Alaskan Peninsula.

A Damn Wreck

Pete Powell

My good friend, Pete Powell, is a professional guide in the Texas Hill Country and a native of Rocksprings, Texas. He told me this priceless hunting story.

It was in the spring, after deer season, when we took these hunters hog hunting (domestic hogs gone wild). These are not considered game animals, so you can hog hunt at any time of year and you do not need a license. We had these German hunters and we were on a hog hunt with dogs in Pearsall, Texas. We were on horseback.

The dogs bayed the hog (there were four or five dogs) into a white brush thicket with only one trail in and one trail out.

O.K., me and my boss, Roy Angermiller of Uvalde and our client went to the opening of the trail. We left the other 3 or 4 clients holding the horses. When we looked down the trail, the hog saw us and was charged by the dogs. When he came down the trail, there was nowhere for him to go.

We could not let the clients shoot because of the dogs. We could not let the hog get to the clients because he would harm them. Their tusks can cut you all the way to the bone.

The client ran and me and Roy went the same way so the hog would come after us. So when the hog broke through the opening, all of the horses the clients were holding scattered, they were so scared. They were adios.

Roy tripped and fell on his back and the hog ran up his chest. I had my 41 Magnum pistol pulled, but I couldn't shoot the hog because he was on top of Roy.

It scared the s_ _ _ out of me and I wasn't even under the hog!

The whole time I'm yelling to the clients, "Do not shoot!" Everybody's around. The dogs, the clients, the hog. I'm so afraid someone's going to get hurt.

Were the clients scared? "Oh s_ _ _ yes!" The one that says he's the biggest hunter is the first to run!

As Roy fell, he drew his Smith and Wesson 41 Magnum pistol. As the hog ran up his chest, he stuck the barrel between his front legs and pulled the trigger.

The hog looked up and saw all the clients standing there and peeled off to go on and get them. He ran about 5 steps and kicked over dead.

He weighed about 300 pounds with 4½-inch long teeth. The hog was a crossed Russian and domestic gone wild.

This 1200-pound Wyoming moose with a 52-inch spread was taken on the Fleming-Barbour hunting range south of Jackson Hole, Wyoming.

Sheep Hunting in Wyoming
A Quest for the Rocky Mountain Bighorn
Barry Barbour

Very few Bighorn Sheep permits are issued in the state of Wyoming. I applied for a permit every year for 9 years and finally drew a license for one in 1973.

I booked my hunt with Charlie Peterson, Jr., who is regarded as one of the foremost outfitter/guides in all of Wyoming with an especially fine success rate of hunting sheep. Charlie's hunters with permits had about 100% success rate in getting their sheep.

I arrived in Jackson Hole in October to hunt sheep only because I had also hunted in Alaska that fall with my most successful hunt of all (see related story). I really was not planning to go to Wyoming because I was not expecting to get a license. I was greatly surprised when I received it.

Bighorn Sheep, killed in Wyoming

We did not set up a camp, just hunted each day and stayed in town since the area was not far from town. Charlie had seen some rams on the Sleeping Indian, a well known 11,000-foot mountain landmark so named because it looks like an Indian sleeping, head dress and all. **We were glassing from across the canyon cause Charlie wanted to see if we could spot the rams before we rode our horses over to the area.** We glassed for two days and saw some sheep but none were rams. So Charlie said that we might as well go on over there because the sheep were there, but they were down in the timber where you could not see them.

We rode our horses over and Charlie brought another guide over to bring our horses back down since we were going to walk down into the timber.

So we started walking down to the timber very carefully. When we had gone about a ½ mile, Charlie was walking along and found a fresh cud (a cud is grass a sheep chews and spits out). Charlie whispered to me that the sheep were not very far.

I was walking a little ahead of Charlie and I looked over a little embankment and I saw a nice ram right down below. I whispered to Charlie, "There's a ram down below." Charlie replied, "Is it legal?" I said "it was more than legal." To be legal, the horns must be a three-quarter curl or longer. There were several rams in the bunch and this one was the largest.

Without saying anymore, I shot the ram about 60 yards away with my 7mm Remington Magnum. I shot quickly because they are very spooky and I knew if they saw us or smelled us they would be gone in an instant.

We went down to where the ram was and Charlie was very excited; so was I. It was a very nice sheep with a 36-inch curl.

After 9 years, the quest was over and well worth the wait.

Barry Barbour killed this 275-pound Audad sheep with a 34-inch curl at Valdena Farms, Sabinal, Texas. It is still listed in the Rowland Ward International Record Book.

FRUITED LEG OF JAVELINA OR WILD HOG

1 javelina or wild hog leg
2 (10 ounce) jars peach or pineapple preserves or orange marmalade
¼ cup vinegar
2 tablespoons prepared mustard
1 teaspoon Worcestershire sauce
Dash hot sauce
6 cups hot fluffy rice
¾ cup whole cashew nuts
⅓ cup fresh parsley, chopped

- Cook javelina or wild hog on barbecue pit until nearly done. Combine preserves, vinegar, mustard, Worcestershire sauce and hot sauce and mix well.

- Baste frequently with marinade to glaze. Pork should cook to internal temperature of 170°.

- Toss rice, nuts and parsley together. Place leg of javelina or wild hog on serving platter and surround with rice. Serve with sauce. Yield: 6 to 8 servings

Tip: *Alternate meat choice: Whole pork loin*

The variety of big game found in Texas is exceptional and includes whitetail and mule deer, wild hogs, javelina, desert bighorn sheep, pronghorn antelope and alligator.

Record-Class Trophies

Barry Barbour stands with elk killed on the Fleming-Barbour Big Game Outfitters hunting area outside of Jackson Hole, Wyoming.

This Boone and Crockett record-class Alaskan moose weighed in at more than 2000 pounds and had a 70-inch spread. It was killed by Barry Barbour on the Alaskan peninsula. Younger son of Barry and Judy, Barry Gorden, steadies the moose head.

A

Record-Class Trophies

Hunting guide Tommy Toolsen, third-generation Jackson Hole native, sits with his 7-point mule deer buck. It had a spread of 34½ inches and weighed over 300 pounds. It missed the Boone and Crockett record book by 2 points.

Warren Fleming, Barry Barbour's hunting buddy and partner in Fleming-Barbour Big Game Outfitters, sits with one of their hunters behind a 6 by 6-point bull elk killed on the Fleming-Barbour hunting range.

Record-Class Trophies

Lifelong friend, Mike Burnside of Bay City, Texas holds the 6-point bull elk taken at the Fleming-Barbour hunting range. The elk weighed more than 750 pounds.

This outstanding trophy elk with a 50-inch spread was killed by Blain Lee on the Fleming-Barbour hunting range.

C

Record-Class Trophies

*Pat Jordan, subject of
Outdoor Life's article
"A Most Unusual Guide"
highlighting Texas Safaris
in Brookshire, Texas, sits
with the mule deer taken
on the Fleming-Barbour
hunting range.*

*Lifelong friend, Jerry
Whitfield of Bay City, Texas
poses with his 6-by-6 bull
elk taken on the Fleming-
Barbour hunting range.*

D

Record-Class Trophies

Barry Barbour shot this Boone and Crockett record class Alaskan moose with a 70-inch spread at Lake Iliamna, Alaska.

Barry Barbour killed this Boone and Crockett record class Barren Ground Caribou in Alaska. The Boone and Crockett score was 421Š. It was the largest caribou killed in Alaska in 1969. The trophy had a 60-inch spread.

E

Record-Class Trophies

Barry Barbour had more than 100 big game trophies during his hunting career. Boone and Crockett and Rowland Ward trophies are on display at Cabela's store in Owatonna, Minnesota, just outside Minneapolis.

This record-class mule deer was killed on the Fleming-Barbour hunting range.

Barry Barbour killed this 275-pound Audad sheep with a 34-inch curl on Valdena Farms, Sabinal, Texas. It is still listed in the Rowland Ward International Record Book.

Barry Barbour took this record-class Barren Ground Caribou with double shovel on the Alaskan peninsula.

This is another record-class Barren Ground Caribou taken by Barry Barbour with hunting outfitter Ray Loesche on the Alaskan peninsula.

F

Record-Class Trophies

A 4 x 8-foot sheet of plywood was used to hold many of the trophies. The point count used for elk in this cookbook is the number of points on 1 side, a system used in the western states.

This Boone and Crockett record-class Alaskan moose with a 65-inch spread weighing over 2000 pounds was killed by Barry Barbour with noted big game outfitter Ray Loesche.

This Dall sheep had a 36-inch curl and was killed in Alaska by Barry Barbour with hunting outfitter Ray Loesche.

Barry Barbour killed this 6 by 7-point bull elk in the Jackson Hole, Wyoming area with outfitter, Charlie Peterson.

This Boone and Crockett record-class Barren Ground Caribou was killed by Barry Barbour with noted outfitter, Ray Loesche, on the Alaskan peninsula.

Barry Barbour killed this 6-point bull elk while hunting with well known outfitter, Charlie Peterson, in the Jackson Hole area.

G

Record-Class Trophies

Hunting stories about many of these record-class trophies are throughout this cookbook. See Table of Contents on page 9 for a complete listing.

This large Wyoming elk was taken by Barry Barbour with outfitter Charlie Petersen.

This Boone and Crockett record-class Barren Ground caribou with double shovel and 44 points was killed by Barry Barbour on the Alaskan peninsula.

Rocky Mountain goat killed by Barry Barbour near Cordova, Alaska.

Barry Barbour killed this Boone and Crockett record-class Barren Ground caribou in Alaska.

Another Boone and Crockett record-class Barren Ground caribou was killed by Barry Barbour in Alaska.

H

GRILLED HOG ROAST WITH A NICE LITTLE ORANGE GLAZE

4 pound leg of wild hog, sheep or boneless pork loin
4 garlic cloves, cut in slivers
1 tablespoon dried rosemary

ORANGE GLAZE:

¼ cup orange marmalade
⅓ cup fresh orange juice
2 tablespoons grated orange rind
⅓ cup honey
1 cup robust red wine
¼ cup Creole mustard
2 tablespoons chili sauce
¼ cup oil
¼ teaspoon red pepper

- Make slits at intervals in leg of wild hog, sheep or pork loin. Insert garlic slivers in slits.

- Combine rosemary with a little salt and pepper. Rub into roast.

- In small saucepan, combine all glaze ingredients and set aside.

- Prepare barbecue grill. Cook leg on grill, covered, for 45 minutes. Baste frequently with glaze.

- Turn, cook additional 45 minutes and baste frequently with sauce to glaze meat.

- Pork should be cooked to internal temperature of 170°. Let stand slightly. Slice and serve hot with reserved glaze. Yield: 6 to 8 servings

SLEEPING INDIAN WILD GAME CHOPS

6 (1-inch thick) chops of bighorn sheep, wild hog, elk, deer, antelope, javelina
2¼ cups marinade
Oil

MARINADE:

¼ cup lime or lemon juice
½ cup orange juice
½ cup vinegar
2 cups apple cider
1 teaspoon tomato bouillon granules with chicken flavor
1 bunch green onions with tops, sliced
1 carrot, chopped
2 ribs celery with leaves, chopped
1 garlic clove, minced
2 tablespoons fresh parsley, minced
1 bay leaf
1 fresh or canned jalapeno pepper, seeded, chopped

- Mix all marinade ingredients: Yield: 4½ cups.

- Use 2¼ cups marinade to pour over chops for several hours and turn occasionally. Drain, pat dry and season with salt and pepper.

- In heavy skillet, heat oil and sear chops on each side. Lower heat and cook until done. Add a little marinade to moisten while cooking. Yield: 3 or 4 servings

Tip: Alternate meat choice: Beef, pork or lamb chops

THE GREATEST BIRTHDAY OF ALL!

Barry Barbour

My younger son, Barry Gorden, and his best friend, Kent Savage, sat on the end of the sofa in our trophy room from the age of six or seven looking at the Boone and Crockett Record Book and dreaming of killing a bear someday.

In the State of Wyoming, you have to be 14 years old to hunt. The summer of 1976 we were in Jackson Hole and Kent and Donald's friend, Harry Norris, had come with us.

Barry Gorden celebrated his 14th birthday on June 4th by proudly purchasing his bear permit. My partner, Warren, and Barry Gorden left Jackson Hole to hunt in Shoal Creek. The weather was cold and snowy. It had been snowing every day for three weeks. Warren had previously been to camp and had put out a bear bait hoping to entice a bear out of hibernation.

Barry Gorden, younger son of Barry and Judy Barbour, killed this black bear on his 14th birthday at the Fleming-Barbour hunting range. It was the second largest bear killed in Wyoming that year. It weighed more than 600 pounds and squared 6' 8".

Barry Gorden and Warren rode their horses to the site and found a bear curiously engaged in dinner. Warren told Barry Gorden to kill the bear.

As a matter of fact, he bluntly said, **"Barry Gorden, if you miss that bear, I'm going to kick your a _ _!"** Barry Gorden raised his 30-06 rifle and looked through the scope, as the bear was feeding on the bait.

He took aim and dropped the bear. He and Warren rode over to the bear and saw how big the bear was, **a huge trophy black bear that was the second largest killed in the state that year.** We thought for a while that it was going to be first. We had the bear mounted life-size on all fours, which he proudly displays in his home.

His friend, Kent, turned 14 on June 20th and although he didn't get a bear on his birthday like Barry Gorden did, he did get one.

This exciting day is still memorable to all of us and was truly the birthday gift of a lifetime.

As Barry Gorden and Warren returned home that night, cold and weary, but so excited, I said, **"Barry Gorden, you are a very fortunate young man!"**

Warren Fleming (right) helps a hunter hold the horns of a 10-point mule deer killed at Fleming-Barbour hunting range.

There's a Bear Coming Down the Freeway

Judy Barbour

Barry had his Alaskan brown bear mounted life-size by **Carter Hood** of Hood Taxidermy in Houston. One day, many months later, Carter called to say the bear was ready for him to pick up. I let the boys miss school to go with him to Houston because I thought it would be educational and exciting for them. At the time, Barry had a Chevrolet El Camino.

The boys and Barry drove 78 miles from Bay City to Houston. They got to Carter's and carefully loaded the bear in the bed of the El Camino and tied it securely. **The bear stood about 8 feet tall, mounted life-size as if he were coming after you.**

They started home down Hwy. 59 (now Interstate 59), about 4:30 p.m., during the peak of the traffic congestion when everyone was getting off from work. At this time it was the craze for everyone to have CB radios in their vehicles. The boys said drivers were almost wrecking their vehicles when they saw a bear going down the highway and the CB's were all jammed with people saying, "there's a bear going down the freeway and it's not a "smokey" bear, which at that time made reference to a highway patrolman.

Needless to say, the boys have never forgotten this day and I wish that I had gone along too!

This black bear taken by Barry Gorden Barbour stood tall in the trailer as it rode from the taxidermist in Houston to its new home in Bay City. Read "The Greatest Birthday of All" and "There's a Bear Coming Down the Freeway" for details.

My Wyoming Black Bear Hunt

Barry Barbour

Before I got my hunting business, I hunted many years with Keith Stilson and Charlie Peterson, Jr. In the fall of 1974, I went bear hunting with Charlie. We drove across Teton Pass, a 10,000-foot pass, from Wyoming into Idaho and then back into Wyoming on the western side of the Teton Mountain Range. We hunted up Moose Creek where Charlie had previously put bear bait out. He had been checking the bait and said that a bear had been feeding off of it.

We hunted there several days and no bear. We got there on the third day about 3 p.m. and walked about a mile to the bear bait site. We settled down in a blind consisting of a pile of logs that Charlie had assembled.

We had been waiting quietly for a couple of hours when we saw this huge black bear coming cautiously toward the bait. He

Kent Savage (right) stands with Warren Fleming and holds a 450-pound black bear he killed at Fleming-Barbour hunting area outside of Jackson Hole, Wyoming. It squared 6 feet.

had his nose up in the air testing the wind. (A black bear cannot see very well, but their sense of smell is very acute.)

Charlie whispered to me that it was a very, very large bear. I took my 7mm Remington Magnum and carefully laid it across a log. I looked through the scope at the cross hairs. **I put the cross hairs right behind his shoulder and squeezed off.** The bear dropped in his tracks. We got up out of the blind and eased

Bay City, Texas native and lifelong friend, Irvine Savage, with his black bear killed with Fleming and Barbour.

over very carefully to make sure he was dead and Charlie exclaimed that I had really gotten a trophy black bear. I did not really know how good it was.

As it turned out, **it was the largest black bear killed in the state of Wyoming that year and won the award given annually by the state of Wyoming.** The bear squared 6 feet 8 or so inches and weighed 500 to 600 pounds. The bear's skull measured 19 inches and was just one inch shy of qualifying for the Boone and Crockett Record Book.

Rocky Mountain Bighorn Sheep are mainly in the Rocky Mountains of North America. They stay above the timberline on grassy slopes or move to lower elevations with more grass and less snow. In the winter a large herd of bighorn sheep may be found in the Upper South Fork of the Shoshone River near Cody, Wyoming. Bighorn sheep are known for their spectacular mating ritual of butting horns during the rutting season.

Bearly a Surprise:
Not All Tall Tales Come from Texas

Barry Barbour

One of my lifelong friends and schoolmates, Dr. Charles Shoultz, Jr. from Bay City, Texas, is a well known heart specialist in Waco, Texas. His father, Dr. Charles Shoultz and my father, Dr. J. Lane Barbour, were colleagues in Bay City. Charles and his family came up to Jackson Hole one summer and we took them on a pack trip. They had a fantastic time.

Three of his colleagues in Waco, Dr. Wayne Falcone, a heart specialist, Dr. Jansson and Dr. Joleff, a psychiatrist, wanted to come hunting with me one year. They all sent in their applications for permits and they all drew elk and deer both. Dr. Joleff had a bear permit, too. The bear license was not on a draw, you could just purchase a license at the Wyoming Game and Fish.

We picked up the doctors at the hotel. In addition to rifle hunting, we found out they were all black powder enthusiasts.

We rode from Jackson Hole down through the Hoback Canyon to Shoal Creek. The doctors exclaimed about the majestic country and asked some questions about hunting. **At night we had a bear bothering our meat rack where we had all our fresh meat.** Dr. Joleff said that he sure would like to kill the bear with his black powder

Dr. Jim Joleff holds the black powder muzzle loader he used to take this 400-pound black bear. Dr. Joleff shot the bear from the cook tent at the Fleming-Barbour hunting camp.

116

muzzle, so I took a coffee can and put about 4 or 5 small rocks in it and hung it off of one of the elk quarters with wire so when the bear would raise up to try to get the elk quarter we'd hear the can rattle and we would know where the bear was. The meat rack was about 30 yards from the door of our cook tent.

Warren backed his pickup truck up by the guide's tent, about 50 yards from the meat rack. He turned his lights on and adjusted them to shine on the meat rack.

We ate supper at about 10 o'clock and everybody went to bed except Dr. Joleff, Warren and I. Warren waited in his pickup, Dr. Joleff and I in the cook tent. We knew the bear would be there before very long. **We shut out all the lights and got everything very quiet. It hadn't been 30 or 40 minutes until we heard the can rattle. And then it really started to rattle.** Then we knew the bear was right under the elk quarter trying to pull it down.

I told Dr. Joleff to get ready 'cause Warren was going to turn the lights on. I pulled the tent flap back quietly so Dr. Joleff would have a good view of the meat rack. In just a few seconds, Warren turned the lights on and you could see the bear standing at the meat rack. I told him to shoot it behind the shoulders, which he did and he was elated. It was a 6-foot bear with a beautiful pelt and it did not have any rub. It was a big, beautiful, cinnamon-colored black bear with a good coat. **In October you seldom get a bear without a rub.** (Spring is really the best time to bear hunt, just when they are coming out of hibernation and have healthier coats.)

This is one hunting story that I am sure many people have thought was a "tall tale". All of the doctors filled out on their game and had a wonderful hunt; one that many years later, they continue to enjoy talking about.

Dr. Jim Joleff, Dr. David Jansson and Dr. Wayne Falcone kneel next to the 6-point bull elk killed at Shoal Creek.

SNOWY PEAK BEAR ROAST

1 (5 to 8 pound) bear shoulder or round steak
2 tablespoons bacon drippings

MARINADE:

¼ cup oil
1 bunch green onions with tops, sliced
3 carrots, chopped
1 rib celery, chopped
1 cup rich beef stock or 2 cups beef bouillon
1 cup red wine
1 cup vinegar
8 whole black peppercorns
1 garlic clove, pressed
1 bay leaf
1 teaspoon Italian seasonings
2 tablespoons dijon-style mustard

- Marinade: Saute green onions, carrots and celery in oil until tender. Add remaining ingredients and simmer for 20 minutes.

- In large, tall bowl, place roast and marinade. Refrigerate several hours, turning several times. Drain, pat dry and sprinkle a little salt and pepper over top. Reserve marinade.

- Heat bacon drippings in large skillet. Sear bear roast and brown all over. Season with salt and pepper. Place in roaster and add marinade.

- Cover and cook at 325° for 3 hours and baste frequently with marinade. Slice and serve with pan juices. Yield: 8 servings.

Tip: Alternate meat choice: Beef, pork or lamb roast

HERMIT'S BLACK BEAR ROAST

1 (3 to 4 pound) black bear roast
3 garlic cloves, chopped
Bacon slices
3 onions, quartered
2 teaspoons beef extract

- Make slivers in roast and insert pieces of garlic cloves so flavors will penetrate meat. Salt and pepper to taste.

- Place in roasting pan and lay bacon slices across top of meat. Add quartered onions, beef extract and 2 cups water.

- Cook, uncovered at 325° until tender. Yield: 6 to 8 servings

This 12-point mule deer with a 37½-inch spread was killed at the Fleming-Barbour hunting range on Shoal Creek south of Jackson Hole, Wyoming.

RANCHERS' COUGAR ROAST

1 (4 to 5 pound) cougar shoulder roast
Vinegar, salt, oil, pepper, garlic powder, paprika
4 tablespoons brown sugar
2 garlic cloves, minced
3 onions, sliced
2 apples, cored, quartered
1 cup red wine
1 tablespoon beef stock or 1 teaspoon beef bouillon
  granules
Bacon strips

- Bone roast and trim all fat. Soak overnight in water with vinegar and salt. Next day, remove meat and pat dry. Roll and tie with kitchen string.

- Rub roast liberally with oil, cook in skillet over high heat and brown on all sides.

- Season with salt, pepper, garlic powder, paprika and brown sugar. Place in floured browning bag and surround with garlic, onions and apples.

- Pour in red wine and beef stock. Cover top with bacon slices. Seal bag and place in roaster. Bake at 325° for 2 to 3 hours or until tender and brown. Yield: 4 servings

Tip: *Alternate meat choice: Beef, lamb or pork roast*

HASENPFEFFER ELEGANTE

1 rabbit, cut up
6 slices bacon
Flour
1 garlic clove, minced
2 beef bouillon cubes
½ teaspoon tomato bouillon granules with chicken
  flavor
1½ cups red wine
1 cup sliced fresh mushrooms
3 tablespoons chopped fresh parsley

- Saute bacon until crisp. Remove from pan. Pour
off most of accumulated bacon grease and reserve
2 tablespoons. Dip rabbit parts in seasoned flour
and brown in remaining bacon grease. Deglaze
juices with wine.

- Place meat in casserole. Add seasonings and bouillon
cubes and crush. Sprinkle with tomato granules. Add
crumbled bacon and wine juices. Bake at 375° for
about 1 hour and turn several times to brown. Add
mushrooms during last 30 minutes of cooking. During
last 5 minutes, add parsley. Yield: 4 servings

Tip: *Alternate meat choice: Domestic rabbit or fryer chicken*

TENDER SMOTHERED DOVES

8 doves or quail
3 tablespoons flour
½ cup oil
1 to 2 garlic cloves
1 cup burgundy wine
Wild rice

- Dust doves with flour seasoned with a little salt and pepper. In heavy skillet, lightly brown doves in heated oil with garlic. Add wine and enough water to barely cover.

- Simmer, covered, about 1 to 1 hour 30 minutes or until tender. Thicken juices in pan with a little of remaining seasoned flour. Serve with wild rice. Yield: 4 servings

Tip: Alternate meat choice: Domestic quail or Cornish game hens, quartered

MESQUITE-GRILLED DOVES

12 doves, dressed
Garlic salt, pepper, red pepper
6 jalapenos, canned or fresh, seeded, halved
12 green onions with tops
6 slices bacon
Italian salad dressing

- Season doves inside and out with garlic salt, pepper and red pepper. Stuff each dove with half of 1 jalapeno pepper and 1 green onion, cut in lengths to fit cavity.

- Wrap half slice bacon around dove and fasten with toothpick to hold stuffing. Grill over mesquite wood about 30 minutes, baste with Italian dressing and turn occasionally until done.

Tip: Alternate meat choice: Boneless chicken thighs

EASY BAKED QUAIL

This makes for tender, juicy birds.

8 quail, dressed
1 garlic clove
1 cup Italian salad dressing

- Place dressed quail in large piece of heavy-duty foil. Salt and pepper to taste. Add garlic and Italian dressing.

- Fold foil together securely. Bake at 350° for 1 hour and shake occasionally.

QUAIL EN BROCHETTE
WITH EGGPLANT

½ cup oil
1 teaspoon beef bouillon
¼ cup sherry
1 teaspoon ketchup
1 teaspoon garlic salt
½ teaspoon black pepper
8 to 10 boned quail breasts
1 cup peeled, cubed eggplant

- **Marinade:** Combine oil, bouillon, sherry, ketchup, garlic salt and pepper. Marinate quail breasts 8 hours and turn occasionally.

- Place quail and eggplant cubes alternately on skewers. Broil on charcoal grill until brown, about 25 minutes. Baste frequently and turn while cooking. Yield: 4 servings

MEXICAN-STYLE PHEASANT OR QUAIL

1 pound wild hog sausage links
1 to 2 pheasants, cut up or 12 quail, halved
½ cup chopped onion
1 cup tomato juice
2 cups chicken broth, divided
1 package Mexican rice seasoning mix
¾ cup rice
1 (10 ounce) package frozen peas
1 (2 ounce) jar pimentos, chopped

- Slice sausages and brown in heavy skillet. Remove sausages and reserve drippings.

- Season pheasants or quail with a little salt and pepper. Brown in sausage drippings. Add a little oil, if needed. Drain.

- Add onion, tomato juice and half of chicken broth. Cover and simmer 2 minutes and turn to cook evenly.

- Add seasoning mix, rice and remaining broth. Return to boiling. Reduce heat, cover and simmer 20 minutes longer.

- Add sausage and peas, cover and simmer 5 minutes more or until peas are tender. Top with pimentos and stir to "fluff" rice and blend. Yield: 4 servings

Tip: *Alternate meat choice: Hot pork sausage links and fryer chicken*

Game birds are defined by the birds designated for hunting seasons. They include wild turkeys, dove, quail, pheasant, partridge, ducks and grouse (sage hen).

Sharp-Shooters' Favorite Stuffed Birds

8 quail, 1 turkey, 2 pheasants, 1 goose or 4 ducks
1 onion, chopped
1 green bell pepper, chopped
1 cup chopped celery with leaves
½ pound livers, chopped (chicken, turkey, pheasant, goose or duck)
½ pound bulk wild game sausage
¼ cup butter
2 cups cooked long grain, wild rice
½ cup chicken bouillon
1 teaspoon tomato bouillon granules with chicken flavor
½ cup white wine

- Saute vegetables in butter until tender. Add livers and sausage and brown slightly. Mix with cooked rice.

- Stuff each bird. (If you are preparing turkey, pheasants or goose, double recipe for stuffing.)

- Rub birds with butter and place in shallow roasting pan. Heat chicken bouillon, tomato bouillon and white wine. Pour over birds.

- Roast at 350° until tender and baste with pan juices during cooking. Quail will cook in 1 hour; turkey, 3 to 4 hours; pheasants, 2 hours; goose, 2 hours 30 minutes to 3 hours; and ducks, 2 hours 30 minutes.

Tip: *Alternate meat choice: Domestically raised quail, turkey, goose, ducks or baking chickens*

RANGE RIDER ROASTED PHEASANT

4 pheasants
2 onions, chopped
4 garlic cloves
1 lemon, sliced
Dry white wine
8 bacon slices

- Sprinkle a little salt and pepper over each bird. Inside cavity of each, place 2 teaspoons chopped onion, 1 garlic clove and 1 lemon slice.

- Secure legs and place in pan, breast side up.

- Place 2 strips bacon over each bird.

- Add half bottle dry white wine. Roast at 325° for 1 hour 30 minutes or until tender.

- Add more wine if necessary. Baste often during roasting. Yield: 4 servings

Adult male ring-necked pheasant are easy to identify by the green head, white ring around the neck, pale bill, red circle around the eye, golden plumage with bluish and greenish iridescence with scattered black spots and long, pointed, golden tail feathers.

Adult female pheasant have similar characteristics to other grouse species, but can be identified by a longer, more pointed tail and bare legs. Female grouse have shorter pointed tails with white outer tail feathers, a shorter neck and feathered legs.

BAKED STUFFED PHEASANTS OR QUAIL ELEGANTE

3 pheasants or 12 quail
½ cup (1 stick) butter, melted
¼ cup dry white wine
½ teaspoon garlic salt
Dash pepper, rosemary and thyme

HAM-RICE STUFFING:

1 cup chopped celery with leaves
½ cup chopped fresh mushrooms
½ cup chopped green onions with tops
½ cup (1 stick) butter
3 cups cooked wild or brown rice
1 tablespoon minced fresh parsley
1 cup chopped ham
Salt, pepper, paprika and garlic powder

- **Ham-Rice Stuffing:** Saute vegetables in butter until tender. Add remaining ingredients and mix well. Stuff birds with mixture.

- Close stuffed birds with skewers and tie with string. Combine remaining ingredients and baste birds. Bake pheasants at 350° for 1 hour 30 minutes and cover if they get too brown.

- Bake quail approximately 45 to 55 minutes and baste occasionally. Check for tenderness.

- Cook giblets in 2 cups boiling water. Combine liquid and pan drippings and thicken for gravy. Add chopped giblets and season to taste. Yield: 6 servings

Tip: Alternate meat choice: Chicken

127

CHAMPAGNE PHEASANT

**4 whole pheasants, dressed
3 yellow onions, quartered
1 pound fresh mushrooms, sliced
Salt, pepper, garlic powder
8 slices bacon
1 bottle champagne**

- Stuff pheasant with onions and mushrooms and place breast-side up in large roasting pan. Add a few onions and mushrooms on the outside of the birds.

- Over each pheasant breast, criss-cross 2 slices bacon. Add bottle of champagne.

- Bake uncovered at 350° for 1 hour 30 minutes or until brown. Baste frequently. (If you need more liquid, add chicken broth.)

- Lower oven to 300°, cover with foil and bake additional 45 minutes or until tender. Spoon champagne juices over breasts to serve. Serves 6.

The ring-necked pheasant is native to Asia and was introduced to California in 1857. By the 1880's they were introduced to additional western states. Today it has naturalized across the northern United States from Oregon to New England.

On-the-Border Grilled Pheasant, Duck or Quail, South Texas Style

2 pheasants, 4 small ducks, 12 quail or 3 game hens
Bacon slices

Sassy South Texas Sauce:

¼ cup chopped, green onions with tops
1 garlic clove, minced
1 lemon
2 tablespoons butter or oil
2 tablespoons brown sugar
2 teaspoons dry mustard
1 (10 ounce) can enchilada sauce
2 ounces jalapeno jelly

- **Sassy South Texas Sauce:** Saute onion and garlic in butter or oil until tender, but not brown. Stir in lemon juice, butter, brown sugar and dry mustard and blend smoothly. Stir in enchilada sauce and jalapeno jelly and simmer 15 minutes.

- Season cavity of each bird with a little salt and pepper. Wrap each with bacon slices secured with toothpicks. Place birds on spit, slightly separated and tied securely. Place spit on rotisserie 6-inches above hot coals and turn on motor. Roast until done and baste frequently with sauce.

- Cook pheasants for about 2 hours, ducks and game hens for 1 hour 30 minutes and quail for 1 hour. Test for doneness. Yield: 4 to 6 servings

Works equally well on the electric indoor rotisserie.

Tip: Alternate meat choice: Domestically raised pheasants, ducks, quail, chickens or Cornish game hens

129

BARRY'S HERB-ROASTED PHEASANT OR GROUSE

2 pheasants or grouse
Sprinkling Italian seasonings
Parsley, minced
6 to 8 small new potatoes, cut in half
4 medium carrots, cut in ½-inch pieces
4 ribs celery, cut in ½-inch pieces
1 (14 ounce) can chicken broth
1 (14 ounce) can beef broth

- Rub birds with a little oil. Sprinkle with seasoning. Place in large roaster and surround with vegetables. Add broth one-third the height of birds. Add small amount of water, if necessary.

- Bake uncovered at 350° for 1 hour and baste frequently. Cover and reduce heat to 250° and bake additional 30 minutes. Remove from oven and let stand for 20 minutes before servings. Yield: 4 servings

Tip: Alternate meat choice: Cornish game hens, sage hens or baking hen

The state bird of South Dakota is the ring-necked pheasant and may be found in farmlands with crops of wheat, oats, hay and corn, as well as certain woodlands and wetlands. Their preferred foods include grains, seeds, wild berries and large insects like crickets and grasshoppers.

BAKED GAME BIRDS MAGNIFIQUE

**2 pheasants or ducks, cut up or 12 quail or
  doves, halved**
¼ cup butter
1 (8 ounce) bottle sweet and sour sauce and dressing
1 (16 ounce) can peach slices, drained
1 (16 ounce) can dark sweet cherries, drained
1 onion, sliced
½ cup chili sauce
Hot cooked rice

- Place game birds of your choice, skin side up, in baking
  pan. Season with a little salt and pepper. Drizzle with
  melted butter. Broil to brown.

- Combine sweet and sour sauce, peaches, cherries, onion
  and chili sauce. Spoon over meat. Bake at 325° for 1
  hour or until meat is tender. Serve over hot cooked rice.
  Yield: 4 to 6 servings

Tip: *Alternate meat choice: Chicken fryer, domestic game
  birds or domestically raised rabbit*

BAKED RABBIT MAGNIFIQUE

- Use all the same ingredients for Baked Game Birds
  Magnifique (above) except the game birds. You'll
  love the same sweet, tart taste with rabbit as your
  main ingredient.

BUCK SHOT JOE'S LEFTOVER PHEASANT OR GROUSE

This is an excellent way to serve leftover fried birds.

> **1 (10 ounce) box frozen, chopped broccoli or 1 cup chopped fresh broccoli**
> **2 cups cooked pheasant or grouse, cubed**
> **½ onion, chopped**
> **¼ cup butter or oil**
> **½ (10 ounce) can mushroom soup**
> **1 (8 ounce) jar processed cheese spread**
> **1 (2 ounce) jar chopped pimentos**
> **3 teaspoons slivered almonds**

- Cook frozen broccoli according to package directions or cook fresh broccoli until tender. Drain and arrange broccoli in bottom of shallow 9 x 9-inch casserole.

- Layer pheasant or grouse over broccoli and sprinkle a little salt and pepper over top.

- Saute onion in butter or oil, add mushroom soup, processed cheese spread, pimentos and mix thoroughly. Pour over broccoli-meat mixture.

- Sprinkle with a little paprika (optional) and almonds and bake at 350° for 20 to 25 minutes. Yield: 4 servings

Game birds may be fried, baked, boiled, broiled and breaded and used in casseroles, soups, stews, gumbos and gravies. Most game birds may be prepared the same as chicken. Frying is common for young birds and stewing is common for older birds.

FEATHERS-FLYIN' BAKED SAGE HENS OR GROUSE

2 sage hens or grouse
½ cup (1 stick) butter, divided
2 tablespoons Worcestershire sauce
Dash hot sauce
1 onion, chopped
½ cup red wine vinegar
1 (10 ounce) can beef bouillon
1 cup red wine
1 rib celery with leaves, chopped
1 green bell pepper, chopped

- Rub birds with butter and sprinkle with a little seasoned salt and pepper. Place half butter in cavity of each.

- Combine remaining ingredients. Place birds in roasting pan and add marinade.

- Cook, uncovered, at 350° for 2 hours and baste frequently. Cover and continue to cook 1 additional hour.

- Turn oven to 400° and cook another 20 minutes. Yield: 4 to 6 servings

Tip: Alternate meat choice: Cornish hens or baking chickens

Common names for sage grouse include sage fowl, sage hen, sage cock, sage chicken, spiney-tailed pheasant, spine-tail grouse and cock-of-the-plains. Male sage grouse are sometimes called old toms, turkey buzzards and master-of-the-plains. Female grouse are sometimes called battle hens and brush hens.

ROAST GROUSE ON LIVER CANAPES

2 grouse
3 tablespoons minced green onions
½ teaspoon dried tarragon
¼ cup melted butter, divided
4 bacon strips

CANAPES:

Unsliced white bread
¼ cup butter
Grouse (or chicken) livers, minced
3 tablespoons finely chopped bacon
¼ teaspoon salt
Freshly ground pepper

SAUCE:

2 tablespoons minced onion
1¼ cups beef bouillon
1 tablespoon butter

- Season cavities of birds with a little salt, green onions, tarragon and half the butter. Brush outsides with remaining butter and place bacon slices over breasts of each bird.

- Roast at 400° for 30 to 40 minutes or until done, baste and turn frequently.

- Slice bread ½-inch thick and cut into rectangles the size of grouse. Saute bread on each side in hot butter and add seasonings.

(Continued on next page.)

- Spread mixture on bread rectangles. Arrange on broiler pan and set aside.

- Just prior to serving, place under hot broiler for 1 minute until sizzling. Remove all but 2 tablespoons fat from roasting pan. Add onions and cook 1 minute. Add bouillon and boil rapidly, scrape up pieces and reduce liquid by half. Stir in butter. To serve place grouse on top hot canape and spoon sauce over birds.

GREAT GROUSE

4 to 6 grouse
2 onions, quartered
4 ribs celery, quartered
2 garlic cloves
Butter

- Split grouse through backs. Place in large pot and add water to cover birds. Add onions, celery, garlic and a little salt and pepper. Cover and simmer for 30 minutes or until tender.

- Remove birds from pot and place under broiler. Brush with butter and baste frequently while cooking.

- Broil for 15 minutes and turn once to brown evenly on both sides. Yield: 4 to 6 servings

PEACH BLOSSOM GROUSE OR QUAIL

4 grouse, halved or 12 quail, split
3 cups barbecue sauce
2 onions, chopped
1 (10 ounce) jar peach preserves
2 tablespoons soy sauce
1 (6 ounce) can sliced water chestnuts, drained
2 green bell peppers, sliced
Hot rice

- Place grouse or quail skin side up in large, shallow baking pan. Sprinkle a little salt and pepper over birds.

- Add a small amount of water to bottom of pan to prevent sticking. Combine barbecue sauce, onion, preserves and soy sauce. Spoon over birds.

- Cover and bake at 350° for 30 minutes. Turn birds and spoon additional sauce over birds. Cover and bake another 30 minutes.

- Turn again, skin side up, and coat with remaining sauce. Bake uncovered another 30 minutes.

- Add water chestnuts and bell peppers. Cook for final 10 minutes. The birds should be tender and golden brown. Yield: 6 servings

Bobwhite quail have whistle calls that sound like "bob-bob-white". They prefer farmlands with brushy cover and woodlands at the boundaries of fields.

ORIGINAL BAKED DUCKS IN WINE

6 wild ducks or 4 pheasants
3 onions, quartered
3 apples, quartered
Salt and pepper
1 litre dry white wine
Bacon slices

• Stuff cavity of duck or pheasant with onions and apples. Salt and pepper to taste. Place in roasting pan with half bottle wine.

• Place 2 strips bacon criss-crossed over breast of each duck or pheasant. Bake, uncovered, at 350° for 2 to 3 hours and baste frequently. (Cooking time depends on size of birds.)

• Cover and bake 1 additional hour or until tender. Skim off accumulated fat, if any, and add remaining wine during cooking. Yield: 6 to 8 servings.

Tip: *Alternate meat choice: 3 Long Island ducklings, Cornish hens or baking hens*

This recipe was first published in Elegant Elk, Delicious Deer *by Judy Barbour.*

The state bird of California is the California quail and has a call of three notes "chi-caa-go" with the mid note the highest.

WILD DUCKS BURGUNDY

2 ducks, quartered
2 tablespoons oil
2 tablespoons flour
1 cup beef bouillon
1 cup sliced fresh mushrooms
½ cup burgundy wine
2 tablespoons shallots
½ teaspoon salt
¼ teaspoon black pepper
1 garlic clove
¼ cup minced fresh parsley

- Simmer ducks in large saucepan in small amount of salted water for 30 minutes. Drain. Brown ducks in oil in large skillet. Remove ducks and place in baking dish.

- Blend flour into skillet juices, add bouillon, mushrooms, burgundy, shallots, salt, pepper and garlic. Cook, stirring frequently, until thick and bubbly. Pour sauce over ducks in baking dish.

- Cover and bake at 350° or until tender, about 1 hour 30 minutes. Place ducks on platter, skim off fat and pour sauce over ducks. Sprinkle with parsley and paprika. Yield: 3 or 4 servings

The mallard is one of the easiest bird species to recognize because of its brilliant, iridescent green head. It is found throughout North America in and around wetlands.

Gringo's Spanish Duck

2 to 4 wild ducks
Flour, oil
1 green bell pepper, sliced in strips
1 small jalapeno pepper, seeded, chopped
1 large onion, chopped
1 (16 ounce) can Mexican-style stewed tomatoes,
    broken up
1 garlic clove, minced
½ teaspoon chili powder
2 ounces jalapeno jelly
Fresh parsley or cilantro, minced
¼ cup Spanish olives, sliced

- Cut up ducks. Roll in flour and brown in small amount of oil in large heavy skillet. Remove from pan. Pour off any excess fat and add remaining ingredients, except parsley or cilantro and olives. Heat to combine.

- Place ducks in large casserole dish, top with tomato mixture and bake, covered at 350° for 1 hour to 1 hour 30 minutes and baste frequently. When tender, sprinkle with fresh parsley or cilantro and sliced olives. Yield: 4 servings

Tip: *Alternate meat choice: Long Island ducklings*

    The mallard duck is the ancestor of all domestic duck breeds except the Muscovy duck. Its widespread population has produced some species that are different enough that they have become a separate species or a sub-species. The Hawaiian duck is a separate species as is the Mexican duck found in central Mexico and the southwestern U.S.

BARBECUED WILD DUCK

1 (2½ to 3 pound) wild duck
1 cup (2 sticks) butter
½ cup ketchup
1 tablespoon brown sugar
2 teaspoons prepared mustard
1½ tablespoons lemon juice
1 tablespoon Worcestershire sauce
3 to 4 drops hot sauce
1 garlic clove, minced
1 small onion, chopped

• Split whole duck in half and flatten. In saucepan, combine all barbecue sauce ingredients.

• Simmer, covered for 5 minutes. Place duck, skin side down, on rack in shallow roasting pan.

• Bake at 375° for 1 hour and baste frequently with barbecue sauce. Turn and cook on other side for 1 hour and baste frequently. Yield: 2 to 4 servings

Tip: Alternate meat choice: Long Island ducklings or Cornish game hens

The wild turkey and the Muscovy duck are the only two domesticated birds native to the New World. European explorers took wild turkeys on their return trips from Mexico as early as the 1500's. They were so popular that colonists brought them back when they settled the colonies. And, wild turkeys were an important food source for Native Americans.

GOLDEN-GLAZED BARBECUED DUCKS

These will cook to a beautiful golden brown.

2 large wild ducks or game hens
Salt, pepper, garlic powder and paprika
Celery leaves, onions slices and lemon wedges
¼ cup oil
1 cup dry red wine
2 tablespoons teriyaki sauce
1 lemon
2 garlic cloves, minced
1 tablespoon prepared mustard
1 tablespoon brown sugar
1 teaspoon minced fresh parsley

- Sprinkle body cavities of birds with seasonings and stuff with celery, onion slices and lemon wedges. Skewer birds closed or tie with string.

- Place on rotisserie over hot coals. Prepare sauce by mixing remaining ingredients. Baste birds frequently with sauce while cooking.

- Cooking time is 15 to 20 minutes per pound. Yield: 4 servings

Tip: *Alternate meat choice: Game Hens, Long Island ducklings or Cornish hens*

The mourning dove is one of the 10 most abundant birds in the U.S. despite its popularity with hunters in all parts of the U.S.

ROASTED WILD DUCK

2 (2-3 pound) ducks
1 onion, quartered
2 apples, quartered
Salt and pepper
Blackberry wine
Bacon slices

- Stuff cavity of ducks with onion and apples. Salt and pepper to taste. Add half bottle blackberry wine.

- Place 2 bacon strips criss-crossed over breast of each duck.

- Bake uncovered at 300° for 4 to 5 hours or until tender. Baste often and add more wine if necessary.

Wild turkey populations were greatly reduced in the 19th and 20th centuries and completely wiped out in the northeast U.S. because of over hunting and habitat loss. The success of transplantations of wild turkey has resulted in growing populations in 49 states.

ROASTED WILD GOOSE

1 cup chopped celery with leaves
1 cup chopped green onions with tops
½ cup chicken broth
1 teaspoon tomato bouillon granules with
    chicken flavor
2 (12 ounce) packages spicy boudin sausage
2 onions, quartered
1 apple, quartered
1 (5 to 7 pound) wild goose
Oil

- Saute celery and green onions in small amount of oil until tender. Add broth, bouillon granules, a little salt and pepper and simmer to blend flavors. Cool slightly.

- Remove casing from boudin, break up and combine with sauteed vegetables.

- Stuff goose alternately with 2 onion quarters, 2 apple quarters and boudin mixture. Oil goose lightly and add a little salt and pepper.

- Place in roasting pan, breast side up, and surround with additional onions and apples. Place bacon slices over goose breast to cover. Add wine and beef extract to pan.

- Bake at 350° for 3½ to 4 hours, baste frequently and add more wine, if needed. Turn to brown evenly. Cover, if necessary, to prevent excessive browning. Yield: 4 to 6 servings

Tip: *Alternate meat choice: Domestically-raised goose*
    or turkey

MARSALA-GLAZED GOOSE OR WILD TURKEY

1 (10 pound) wild goose or wild turkey
1 cup pineapple juice
1 cup marsala wine
¼ cup orange-flavored liqueur
1 orange, sliced
Orange zest
2 oranges, peeled, sliced into cart wheels
2 kiwi fruits, peeled, sliced into circles
Maraschino cherries

- Remove giblets from bird and sprinkle a little salt and pepper over bird. Place in roasting pan.
- Combine pineapple juice, wine, liqueur, sliced orange and orange zest. Pour over goose.
- Roast at 350° for 4 to 5 hours, basting occasionally, and turn to brown evenly. Add more wine or water, if necessary.
- Spoon off any excess fat during cooking. (Cover, if necessary, so it will not get too brown.)
- Place on platter and decorate with orange cartwheels, top each with 1 kiwi fruit slice and 1 maraschino cherry. Yield: 6 to 8 servings

Tip: *Alternate meat choice: Domestic goose, turkey or Cornish hens*

Not all ducks migrate annually but some do make long migrations from breeding grounds in Canada to wintering grounds in southern U.S., Mexico and Venezuela.

CAJUN-STYLE FRIED WILD TURKEY

Fry the whole turkey! It will be black and crispy on the outside and juicy and moist on the inside.

1 (15 to 20 pound) wild turkey
Red or cayenne pepper
3 tablespoons or more hot sauce
1 (16 ounce) bottle Italian dressing
5 tablespoons Worcestershire sauce
5 gallons peanut oil

- Sprinkle turkey liberally with salt, pepper and red pepper inside and out. Place in heavy-duty foil. Mix hot sauce, Italian dressing and Worcestershire sauce.

- With large syringe, inject mixture into turkey, just under the skin. Carefully pat into place. Wrap turkey in foil and place in refrigerator several hours to marinate. Remove 30 minutes prior to cooking.

- On large outdoor burner, place large pot with basket. Heat oil until very hot (350°) and lower turkey into hot oil. Cook 3 minutes per pound.

Tip: *Alternate meat choice: Domestically raised turkey*

At least 4000 years ago, early inhabitants of what is now America made "calls" from turkey wingbones to mimic their sounds to draw them in close enough to catch and kill.

BARRY'S WILD CAJUN TURDUCKEN
"What on earth is turducken?"

It is a unique Cajun creation, a composite of boned turkey, duck and chicken placed one on top of the other and each separated with layers of Cajun cornbread or boudin stuffing (dressing). It is then rolled, cooked, sliced and enjoyed.

This imaginative Cajun creation has received raves at many of our catering events as well as in our restaurants. It may be served with crab rolls, seafood gumbo, wild rice pilaf, zucchini almandine and New Orleans pralines for an authentic Cajun feast.

> **1 large wild turkey**
> **2 wild ducks**
> **1 (2½-3 pound) chicken**
> **Chicken broth or stock**
> **White wine**
> **Salt**
> **Cayenne**
> **Black pepper**
> **Creole Cajun seasonings**
> **Dressing**

- Bone all birds and lay meat flat on cutting board. Season birds with salt, pepper and Creole or Cajun seasonings.

- Use turkey for first layer and top with one-fourth of dressing. Lay meat from duck on top of dressing and top with one-fourth of dressing. Repeat layers with second duck and chicken.

- Roll stack in jellyroll fashion and tie with kitchen string at intervals. Bake at 350° until tender.

- Let it stand for a few minutes before slicing. Slice across all birds and stuffing in a pinwheel style and serve.

WILD TURKEY LEGS IN RED WINE

4 wild turkey legs
1 tablespoon butter
1 tablespoon olive oil
4 to 5 green onions with tops, sliced
1 carrot, minced
2 tablespoons flour
½ bottle (12 ounces) red wine
¾ cup beef bouillon
1 garlic clove, minced
1 bay leaf

- Heat butter and oil in heavy skillet or Dutch oven. Brown turkey legs and remove. Add green onions and carrots and cook over low heat until soft, about 3 minutes. Stir in flour and cook until brown, about 3 minutes.

- Add wine, bouillon, a little salt and pepper and remaining seasonings. Add turkey legs, cover and simmer until very tender, about 1 hour 30 minutes, turn and baste occasionally.

- Remove turkey and cook liquid until it reaches thickness of gravy. Slice turkey meat from bones and discard bones. Serve with rich gravy. Yield: 4 servings

Tip: *Alternate meat choice: Domestic turkey legs*

An adult turkey has 5,000 to 6,000 feathers that cover the body. Turkeys can run as fast as 25 mph and fly as fast as 55 mph.

HUNTERS' HARVEST FEAST

A bunch of hunters pool their harvest for a real feast.

5 pounds mixed wild game
(elk, deer, sheep, moose, antelope, pheasant, quail, wild turkey, sage
hens, grouse, ducks, doves, rabbits, pork loin, sausage links, etc)
Oil
2 carrots, diagonally sliced
1 Spanish onion, quartered
1½ cups fresh parsley, divided
2 stalks celery with leaves, diagonally sliced
2 garlic cloves, minced
2 lemons, juiced
1 cup hearty burgundy wine
1 pound tomatoes, peeled, chopped
½ teaspoon crushed red pepper
1 cup beef broth
6 thick slices French bread

- Cut game into bite-size pieces. Split quail and bone dove breasts. Brown meat and birds with oil in large Dutch oven or large, heavy skillet. Add vegetables and garlic and saute about 5 minutes.

- Add lemon juice, wine and fresh tomatoes and continue cooking covered, about 45 minutes, stirring occasionally. Season with a little salt and pepper and crushed red pepper. Add broth and continue cooking, covered, until all meats are tender and stock reduces.

- When casserole is ready to serve, preheat oven to 400°. Place bread on baking sheet and toast on each side until brown. Place 1 slice of toasted bread in each of 6 small casseroles and ladle game mixture into each. Sprinkle with fresh parsley (optional) and serve hot. Yield: 6 to 8 servings

Tip: *Alternate meat choice: Beef, veal, pork, chicken, turkey, domestic rabbit, quail, ducks and geese*

Big Texan Catches Big Fish!

Barry Barbour

In August 1973, my family and I flew to Honolulu, Hawaii for a summer vacation where we stayed at the new Sheraton Waikiki.

I wanted to go fishing for marlin so I went down to the docks to see what was available. I chartered a 32-foot Bertram named "Magic Time". Little did I know what that was going to mean to me! The next morning my older son, Donald, age 13, and I went fishing. Barry Gorden, the younger son, did not go because he got seasick.

It was nearing the end of a good fishing season and the captain said it had been a slow season. **We went out about 10 or 15 miles offshore, trolling all morning and didn't have a single knockdown.**

Donald was starting to feel a little bit seasick. About that time we had two knockdowns simultaneously. I got in the fighting chair and the captain handed me one of the rods and he took the other one. I started reeling the fish in. **We did not know for sure what we had on the line.** The fish did not jump, so we did not think it was a marlin. When I got the fish close to the boat, we could tell that it was a big, yellowfin tuna.

I carefully reeled the fish close to the boat and the mate took the gaff and gaffed the fish. He and I brought the fish on board. Donald got so excited that he forgot all about being seasick.

As soon as I got that fish on board, I took the rod and I brought another yellowfin tuna up close to the boat, which we

...these two yellowfin tuna were the largest caught in all the Hawaiian waters that year – 241 pounds and 210 pounds, respectively.

gaffed also. As it turned out, **these two yellowfin tuna were the largest caught in all the Hawaiian waters that year – 241 pounds and 210 pounds, respectively.**

Of course, the captain was very excited and got on the radio, telling them back in port about our magnificent catch.

The captain and I had visited on our way out fishing. I had, just in conversation, casually told him that I was a big game hunter and fisherman and that **I had about 100 trophies in my home in Texas.**

Being the modest person that I am, I was surprised when the news was out on all the other fishermen's radios. "Big Texan Catches Big Fish – the largest in all the Hawaiian waters, this season. Big hunter with 100 trophies!" Needless to say, Donald was so excited and very proud of me.

As we traveled back to the dock, a big crowd awaited us, along with the radio station crew broadcasting live, as they interviewed me about catching the big fish. The television station wanted me to be on television the next day, however, we were leaving, so I declined.

It was a very eventful trip that I will never forget. It was truly a "Magic Time".

Yellowfin tuna is a fast swimmer living in tropical and sub-tropical waters. They eat crustaceans, other fish and squid. They can be 90 inches long and weigh up to 440 pounds. The main body is a dark blue metallic color with a silver underbelly and yellow dorsal and anal fins.

ITALIAN-STYLE BAKED FISH

1 cup sliced green onions with tops
¼ cup oil
1 (16 ounce) can stewed, Italian-style tomatoes,
    broken up
1 garlic clove, minced
½ teaspoon Italian seasonings
1 (3 ounce) jar Spanish olives, sliced
2 tablespoons capers, drained
1 teaspoon minced flat-leaved Italian parsley
3 pounds "Catch-of-the-Day" fish fillets or steaks

- Saute onions in oil until soft. Add tomatoes and simmer
  5 minutes. Stir in remaining ingredients.

- Place fish in large flat baking dish. Top with sauce. Bake
  at 350° for 35 to 40 minutes and baste while cooking.
  Yield: 6 servings

Tip: *Alternate fish choice: Any fresh market fish fillets
  or steaks*

About 83% of Americans eat canned tuna for lunch. It
is the only seafood regularly eaten at lunch.

WHOLE FISH BAKED OVER-THE-COALS

3 pounds whole salmon, red snapper, tuna, halibut
   with head and tail, cleaned
Oil
4 lemons, divided
1 to 2 onions, sliced
1 large tomato, chopped
Creole seasonings to taste
¼ cup soy sauce
1 teaspoon Worcestershire sauce
2 lemons, sliced

- Start fire and let coals get hot. Place fish on large piece of heavy-duty foil, shiny side up. Lightly oil fish. Sprinkle with juice of two lemons and top with onion and tomatoes.

- Season with Creole seasonings, soy sauce, Worcestershire and parsley (optional). Top with slices from remaining lemons.

- Wrap fish securely in foil. Place on hot coals and cook 45 to 55 minutes. Unwrap and serve immediately with juices. Yield: 6 servings

Tip: Alternate fish choice: Works equally well with any whole fresh market fish.

Salmon is relatively healthy because of its high protein and Omega-3 fatty acids. Salmon has a high content of niacin, vitamin B6, vitamin B12 and phosphorus.

POLYNESIAN-STYLE SALMON STEAKS

¼ **cup oil**
¼ **cup fresh lime juice**
1 tablespoon soy sauce
2 teaspoons honey
Creole seasonings
Lime slices
4 (6-8 ounce) salmon steaks or fillets

- Combine oil, lime juice, soy sauce, honey, Creole seasoning and a dash of water. Set steaks in large flat dish.

- Pour marinade over steaks, cover and refrigerate several hours. Turn several times to coat evenly.

- Prepare grill, drain fish and reserve marinade. Grill over medium hot coals for 10 to 12 minutes and turn to brown. Brush with marinade while cooking. Serve hot with 1 lime slice each. Yield: 4 servings

Tip: *Alternate fish choice: Red snapper, orange roughy, halibut, catfish, swordfish, tuna, cod, sea bass*

Salmon may be found in the Pacific and Atlantic Oceans, the Great Lakes and the Kamchatka Peninsula in Russia. Salmon are born in fresh water, migrate to the ocean and return to fresh water where at least 90% of the time is the same area where they were born. All mature Pacific salmon die within weeks of spawning. How they navigate is still a mystery.

PACIFIC NORTHWEST GRILLED SALMON WITH TARRAGON-MUSTARD SAUCE

4 (6 to 8 ounce) salmon steaks
3 tablespoons unsalted butter
½ cup dry white wine
1 teaspoon dried tarragon
2 teaspoons dijon-style mustard
¼ cup whipping cream

- Grill salmon over medium-hot coals for about 3 minutes per side. (Do not overcook. Fish will be dry.)

- Melt butter in saucepan and add wine, tarragon and mustard.

- Simmer until reduced by one third to one half. Stir constantly and pour in cream. Simmer 1 minute.

- Season with a little salt and white or black pepper. Serve over grilled salmon. Yield: 4 servings

Tip: *Alternate fish choice: Red snapper, orange roughy, halibut, catfish, swordfish, tuna, cod, sea bass, amberjack*

Atlantic salmon is the primary species after which all others are named. The salmon of the Great Lakes is a non-migratory sub-species. Another sub-species is classified as trout.

Fresh Salmon Steaks with Cucumber-Dill Sauce

4 (6 to 8 ounce) salmon steaks
¼ cup butter
1 lemon or lime, juiced
Dash hot sauce
¼ teaspoon paprika

Cucumber-Dill Sauce:

½ pint sour cream
¼ teaspoon hot sauce
1 cup grated cucumber
1 tablespoon fresh dill, snipped

- Combine all ingredients for Cucumber-Dill Sauce. Refrigerate while preparing salmon steaks. Season steaks with a little salt and pepper.

- In small saucepan, melt butter and stir in lemon or lime juice, hot sauce and paprika.

- Pour over steaks in shallow baking dish. Bake at 350° for 25 to 30 minutes. Do not overcook. Serve with sauce. Yield: 4 servings

Tip: Alternate fish choice: Red snapper, orange roughy, halibut, catfish, swordfish, tuna, cod, sea bass, amberjack, wahoo, etc. May also be prepared with fillets of fish rather than steak.

CATCH-OF-THE-DAY FISH STEW

9 large tomatoes, peeled
½ cup thinly sliced green onions with tops
2 serrano chilies, stemmed, seeded, minced
1 cup chopped fresh cilantro
Dash sugar
1 cup dry white wine
1 cup fish stock or clam juice
Creole seasoning
3 pounds assorted fish fillets, cubed
    (halibut, cod, red snapper, sea bass or amberjack)

- Dice tomatoes into ¼-inch cubes. Combine tomatoes, green onions, chilies, (2 hot red chilies, optional) and cilantro in large mixing bowl. Mix well.

- In large heavy stockpot, place tomato-salsa mixture, sugar, wine, fish stock or clam juice, Creole seasoning and a little salt and pepper.

- Bring to slow boil, reduce heat and simmer 10 minutes. Add fish chunks and stir gently. Simmer additional 15 minutes. Adjust seasonings if needed. Yield: 6 to 8 servings

Albacore tuna has white meat, is promoted as the white tuna and sports the nickname "chicken of the sea". It is migratory, constantly on the move and found in cool tropical waters.

PESCADO DE MEXICO

Fish of Mexico

⅓ **cup dry breadcrumbs**
1 small onion, grated
1 green bell pepper, chopped
2 canned pimentos, chopped
½ **cup (1 stick) butter, softened**
1½ **teaspoons chili powder**
1 teaspoon paprika
3 to 4 pounds dorado, blue marlin, sailfish, grouper, tuna fillets or steaks
1 cup white wine

- Blend all ingredients, except fish and wine. Place fillets or steaks in large, shallow baking dish.

- With spatula or flat knife, smooth butter-seasoned mixture on top of each piece of fish.

- Pour white wine in dish and surround fish. Bake at 400° for 25 to 30 minutes. Yield: 6 to 8 servings

Tip: *Alternate fish choice: Any fresh "Catch of the Day" fish fillets or steaks or fresh market fish*

Red snapper is a very popular white fish because it has a firm texture and a sweet, nutty flavor making it great to pair with strong chilies or subtle seasonings. It's very easy to grill whole red snapper because the skin holds the meat together. Matched with lemon slices, butter and seasonings, red snapper on the grill, green banana leaf or cedar plank is exceptional.

JACKSON LAKE MACKINAW OR CUTTHROAT TROUT PROVENÇAL

¼ cup chopped shallots
½ cup chopped bell pepper
⅓ cup olive oil
1 (4 to 6 pound) whole trout
¼ cup fresh lemon juice
3 tablespoons minced fresh parsley
4 tomatoes, peeled, chopped
1 (4 ounce) can tomato sauce
¼ cup sliced stuffed olives
Lemon slices

- Brown shallots and bell peppers lightly in olive oil. Remove from pan. Saute fish in oil and brown on both sides. Place fish in large casserole dish.

- Remove excess oil from skillet and add shallots, bell peppers, a little salt and pepper, lemon juice and parsley. Add tomatoes and tomato sauce. Simmer a few minutes to blend.

- Pour over fish in casserole and bake at 350° for about 15 minutes or until fish flakes easily. Do not overcook. Garnish with stuffed olive slices and lemon slice. Yield: 4 servings

Cutthroat trout include coastal cutthroat, Yellowstone cutthroat, sea trout, lake trout, Clark's trout, red-throated trout and short-tailed trout. The average length is about 17 inches and they can weight up to 17 pounds.

CAMPFIRE BACON-WRAPPED TROUT

There is nothing better than freshly caught, fried Rocky Mountain Trout.

1 (8 ounce) can tomato sauce
6 ounces beer
⅛ cup butter or oil
2 tablespoons lemon juice
2 tablespoons sliced green onions with tops
¼ cup white wine
Salt, pepper, thyme, garlic powder, onion powder to taste
1 bay leaf
1 teaspoon parsley flakes
Pinch brown sugar
6 (about 8 ounces each) rainbow trout, whole, cleaned, scaled

- In saucepan, combine all ingredients except trout. Simmer for 15 minutes to allow flavors to blend and stir occasionally.

- Wrap each fish in 2 slices bacon. Secure with toothpicks. Place on prepared grill and cook 6 minutes per side.

- Brush often with sauce. Serve fish hot with sauce. Yield: 6 servings

Tip: Alternate fish choice: cutthroat, brook or brown trout, any individual-size whole fresh fish

The rainbow and steelhead trout are in the top five most popular sport fish in North America because of the hard fight they make once caught.

TROUT HEMINGWAY, BARBOUR STYLE

Ernest Hemingway, a great hunter and fisherman, knew and wrote about a good pan of fried trout. I think he would have approved of my version. It is perfect for camping out or cooking in the kitchen!

Salt, pepper, garlic powder, paprika
½ cup flour
½ cup yellow cornmeal
½ to ¾ cup butter or oil
Lemon wedges
6 (8 ounce) freshly caught rainbow trout, whole, cleaned, scaled

- In shallow pan combine salt, pepper, garlic powder, paprika, flour and cornmeal and mix thoroughly. In large frying pan, melt butter over medium-high heat or heat oil.

- Moisten each piece of fish slightly with water, dip in seasoned mix and coat sides and cavity of fish. Place in skillet, brown 3 to 5 minutes per side and fry crisply.

- Serve with lemon wedges. (Always remember, do not overcook fish or it will be dry and tough.)
  Yield: 6 servings

Tip: *Alternate fish choice: Cutthroat, brook or brown trout, saltwater trout, catfish, salmon.*

The red snapper has a pinkish, reddish body with pale belly and is found offshore on the continental shelf. They average about 20 pounds, but the Florida record is 46 pounds 8 ounces.

BEER BATTER BASS NUGGETS

Especially good with shrimp, too!

1½ pounds bass fillets
⅓ cup lemon juice
Flour
Peanut oil
Tartar sauce
Lemon wedges

BEER BATTER:

¾ cup flour
1 (12 ounce) beer

- **Beer batter:** Sift together flour and a little salt and pepper. Blend in beer. Let set, covered, in refrigerator for 1 hour. Stir prior to using.

- Cut fillets into 1½-inch strips for fish bites or nuggets. Toss with lemon juice and a little salt and pepper. Let stand, refrigerated, for 30 minutes. Drain fillets.

- Season additional flour with a little salt and pepper and sprinkle over fish to coat. Dip in beer batter.

- Deep fry in hot oil for 2 to 3 minutes. Drain and keep warm until all fish cooks. Serve with tartar sauce and lemon wedges. Yield: 4 servings

Tip: Alternate fish choice: Any fresh catch of fish or market fish fillets

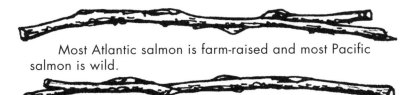

Most Atlantic salmon is farm-raised and most Pacific salmon is wild.

CATCH-OF-THE-DAY BEER-SOAKED FRIED FISH

4 pounds fish fillets
1 to 2 (12 ounce) cans beer
2 cups flour
1 cup yellow cornmeal
1 cup biscuit mix
1 teaspoon seasoned salt
1 teaspoon black pepper
1 teaspoon paprika
Oil
Lemon wedges
Tartar sauce or red sauce

- Rinse fish, pat dry and cut in serving-size pieces. Pour enough beer over fish to cover and soak.

- Mix flour, cornmeal, biscuit mix and seasonings. Place flour mixture in paper or plastic bag.

- Place fish, in batches, in bag and shake to coat thoroughly.

- Fry in hot oil until done and crisp. Do not overcook.

- Drain on paper towels. Serve with lemon wedges, tartar sauce and red sauce. Yield: 6 servings

Rainbow trout and steelhead trout are very similar with their primary difference being the rainbow trout is a fresh water fish and the steelhead is a salt water fish. The average length of the rainbow trout is 18-20 inches and 20-30 inches for the steelhead. The rainbow trout has the most colorful body.

CREOLE-STYLE FRIED FISH NUGGETS

36 individual pieces of fresh fish fillets (bass, trout, red snapper)
1 quart buttermilk
Creole seasoning
⅓ cup butter
⅓ cup oil
3 cups flour

- Soak fish fillets in buttermilk in large, flat pan. Cover and refrigerate several hours and turn to coat evenly. Drain fish and discard milk. Rinse well and pat dry.

- In large heavy skillet, heat butter and oil over medium heat.

- When hot, dredge fish fillet nuggets in flour and coat well. Fry to golden brown.

- Remove and sprinkle with Creole seasonings and keep warm until all cook. Serve hot. Yield: 4 to 6 servings

Tip: *Alternate meat choice: Chicken wings*

Donald Barbour and the Hinton boys with a string of
cutthroat and rainbow trout from Jackson Hole.

CAJUN-MUSTARD FRIED CATFISH

4 pounds catfish fillets or nuggets
Oil
1 cup prepared mustard
2 eggs, well beaten
1 teaspoon hot sauce
1 cup unseasoned fish fry
1 cup yellow corn meal
1 cup flour
1 cup fine breadcrumbs
Creole seasonings
Lemon wedges

- Pat fish dry and set aside. In mixing bowl, combine mustard, eggs and hot sauce. Pour mixture into large flat pan.

- In another bowl, combine all remaining ingredients, except lemon wedges. Pour into another flat baking dish.

- Heat oil in large heavy skillet. Dredge fish fillets or nuggets in mustard mixture and turn to coat all surfaces.

- Dip fish in cornmeal mixture and turn to coat well. Shake off excess.

- Fry in hot oil, a few at a time, until golden brown and crispy, and turn to brown evenly. Serve hot with lemon wedges. Yield: 4 to 6 servings

WHALE TALES' SEAFOOD GUMBO

ROUX:

1 cup flour
1 cup oil

- Make roux by mixing flour and oil in skillet over medium-high heat. Stir, almost continuously, to combine and brown about 45 minutes. Set aside.

GUMBO:

½ cup chopped onion
½ cup chopped celery with leaves
½ cup chopped green bell pepper
½ cup chopped green onions with tops
4 cloves garlic, minced
¼ pound butter
2 (10 ounce) cans beef bouillon
1 tablespoon Worcestershire sauce
1 (16 ounce) can Cajun-style stewed tomatoes
Creole seasoning
4 crabs and claws, cleaned, quartered
2 pounds fresh shrimp, peeled
½ pound fish fillets
½ pint oysters
2 cups sliced, cooked okra
½ cup chopped parsley
Dash filé
Hot fluffy rice

- Saute fresh vegetables and garlic in melted butter for 10 minutes. Add vegetables, 2 quarts water, bouillon, Worcestershire sauce, tomatoes and Creole seasoning to roux mixture. Cook for 1 hour.
- Cut fish in bite-size pieces. Add fish and seafood to gumbo and cook 1 additional hour. Add okra before serving just to heat through. (If you add the okra during cooking, it will be stringy.) Add dash of filé. Serve in bowls over hot rice and garnish with onion tops and parsley. Yield: 8 servings

165

CAPTAIN HOOK'S SEAFOOD CASSEROLE

¾ cup rice
8 ounces fresh crabmeat
1 pound fresh shrimp, cooked, veined, diced
½ pound cooked lobster tail meat, diced
1 bell pepper, chopped
1 onion, chopped
1 cup chopped celery
1 (10 ounce) can cream of mushroom soup
1 teaspoon sweet basil
1 cup mayonnaise
2 cups crushed potato chips or breadcrumbs

- Cook rice according to package directions. Mix rice, crabmeat, shrimp, lobster, bell pepper, onion, celery and soup.

- Add a little salt and pepper and basil. Blend in salad dressing.

- Place mixture in decorative 2-quart casserole dish. Top with crushed potato chips or breadcrumbs. Bake at 350° for 45 minutes. Serves 8

Tip: *You may also divide mixture into 8 scallop shells or ramekins and top with chips or crumb. Bake at 350° for 30 minutes.*

The giant sea bass is found off the coast of California and gets up to 550 pounds although it is rare. The black sea bass name refers to the common name of a species found on the east coast of the U.S.

BAYSIDE CRAB CAKES

4 green onions with tops, finely chopped
6 tablespoons butter
2 pounds cooked crabmeat
½ cup fresh breadcrumbs
½ cup finely crushed cracker crumbs
1½ teaspoons dry mustard
½ teaspoon paprika
2 eggs, beaten
1 tablespoon minced pimentos
Cream
Seasoned cracker crumbs
Oil

- Saute onions in butter until soft. Add crabmeat and set aside. Combine dry ingredients and beaten eggs and mix. Add to crabmeat mixture.

- Fold in pimentos. Stir lightly over medium heat and pour in enough cream to bind together.

- Shape into 6 or 8 crab cakes and roll in seasoned cracker crumbs. Fry in hot oil about 5 minutes per side until done and brown. Drain excess oil and serve hot. Yield: 6 or 8 crab cakes

Shrimp is America's most popular seafood and comes primarily from the Atlantic and Pacific coasts as well as the Gulf Coast.

FROG LEGS PROVENÇAL

¼ cup sliced green onions with tops
1 cup sliced mixed red and green bell peppers
¼ cup olive oil
16 to 20 frog legs
¼ cup fresh lemon juice
3 tablespoons minced fresh parsley
4 fresh tomatoes, peeled, chopped
½ cup tomato sauce
¼ cup white wine
¼ cup sliced Spanish olives
Lemon slices

- Saute onions and bell peppers in olive oil. Remove from pan. Brown frog legs in oil. Remove frog legs and place in large casserole.

- Remove excess oil from skillet and lemon juice, a little salt and pepper and parsley to skillet. Add fresh tomatoes, tomato sauce and white wine. Simmer several minutes to blend.

- Pour over frog legs in casserole and bake at 350° for 35 to 45 minutes or until done. Garnish with Spanish olives and lemon slices. Yield: 4 to 5 servings

Tip: *Alternate meat choice: Chicken wings*

Frog legs are usually pan-fried, deep-fried, sauteed and used in casseroles. They are a favorite dish in France.

Wyoming's Abundant Wild Life

Wyoming has an abundance of magnificent wild game. It has the largest pronghorn antelope and elk herds in the world. Big game animals also include black bears, grizzly bears, mule deer, moose, mountain sheep, lynxes and mountain lions. Small game animals include beavers, badgers, martens, raccoons, foxes, coyotes, wildcats and rabbits. Game birds also abound and include ducks, geese, pheasants, sage hens, grouse and wild turkeys.

Texas Exotics

There are numerous exotic game ranches in the Texas Hill Country where the game adapts well to the habitat. You can hunt wild game species from around the world year round because there is no season and no licenses required.

You will find an abundance of sika and axis deer from China and Japan, black bucks from India, red deer from Europe and New Zealand, white fallow deer from Greece, Audad (Barbary) sheep from the Barbary Coast of Northern Africa, ibex from Nubia, wild turkeys, buffalo, Texas Dalls, Hawaiian sheep and many more.

This coveted game meat can be prepared interchangeably with recipes for similar native North American game species.

Several ranches in the Texas Hill Country that offer the finest exotic game hunting in the United States include the YO Ranch, a 40,000-acre ranch outside Kerrville, Clear Springs Ranch specializing in record-class exotics outside Bandera and the 777 Ranch outside Hondo, a 16,000-acre ranch with 56 species from around the world.

Y.O. Ranch – A Texas Legend

The Y.O. Ranch, located in the beautiful Hill Country of Mountain Home, Texas, is home to North America's largest collection of exotic wild animals. Sika deer from Japan, Nile lechwe from the Sudan, Nilgai antelope from India, European mountain sheep, eland, Australian emus, black buck antelope from Pakistan, rhea from South America, zebras, giraffes, ostriches, oryx, aoudad and others may be found on the ranch.

The ranch was established in 1880 by Captain Charles Schreiner after he immigrated from the Alsace-Lorraine region of France in 1838. He served with the 3rd Texas Infantry during the Civil War. He was a Texas Ranger and also was a banker, merchant and philanthropist. The original ranch had 600,000 acres and he raised cattle, sheep and goats. Today the ranch consists of 40,000 acres and is still a working cattle ranch. It is located west of Kerrville and 60 miles northwest of San Antonio, Texas.

Captain Schreiner first brought the longhorn cattle to the ranch in the early 1880's. Today, the Y.O. is the home of the largest herd of longhorns in the United States. Much credit is given to Captain Schreiner's colorful, ingenious grandson, Charlie III. By 1964 the longhorn breed was near extinction. Few ranches had any longhorns and the largest herd was in a wildlife refuge in Oklahoma. Charlie III, set out to change that, by founding the **Texas Longhorn Breeders' Association**. The first Texas longhorn bull and calf came out of the Y.O. in 1964.

In 1990 Schreiner established the **Exotic Wildlife Association**. It was that year that the Y.O. began importing exotic animals to the ranch for hunting purposes and the ranch is now a hunting mecca for photographers, native game hunters and exotic game hunters from around the world. Hunting is available year round on the ranch.

Five generations of the Schreiner family have lived and worked on the ranch. A true Texas legend lives on at the Y.O. Ranch.

777 Ranch

The 777 Ranch, about 40 miles west of San Antonio and just outside Hondo, Texas, is a 15,000-acre ranch dominated by trophy wild game with more than 50 different species. The 777 (triple 7) has been stocking and raising exotics for more than 30 years and boasts some of the largest trophies in the world.

The 777 has one of the most diverse and highly populated wildlife herds in the world. It also has one of the highest quality whitetail herds in the U.S.

Selective hunting is done safari-style from well-equipped 4-wheel-drive jeeps. Wildlife jeep safari tours are also available and showcase animals from Africa, India, Europe, the Middle East and Asia.

This Rocky Mountain goat was killed by Barry Barbour with noted bush pilot and hunter, Buddy Woods, near Cordova, Alaska.

This Boone and Crockett record-class caribou was killed by Barry Barbour on the Alaska Peninsula.

Clear Springs Ranch

C lear Springs Ranch is one of the finest Texas Hill Country hunting resorts for exotic wild game, whitetail trophy bucks and management whitetail deer. It is located in the heart of the Texas Hill Country outside Bandera, Texas, the "Cowboy Capital of the World".

There are over 30 exotic wild game species including addax, aoudad, axis, barasingha, blackbuck, black Hawaiian, blesbok, bobcat, bongo, buffalo, Catalina goat, Corsican, dama gazelle, eland, elk, fallow deer, gemsbok, wild hogs, hybrid ibex, kudu, mouflon, nilgai, Nubian ibex and Pere David deer, red deer, red sheep, sable, scimitar oryx, sika, Texas Dall, wild turkey, waterbuck, white-bearded wildebeest, zebra and whitetail deer.

Hunting is year round on this 1,120-acre ranch with another 2,000-acre ranch available for seasonal hunting of quail, dove, turkey and wild hogs. Terrain is typical Hill Country land with rough brush in the hills and valleys and large oaks that dominate the landscape.

Clear Springs Ranch is a world-wide favorite destination for hunters seeking wild game trophies and is a Texas experience not soon forgotten.

This large mule deer was killed by Barry Barbour at the Fleming-Barbour hunting range on Shoal Creek, Wyoming.

2005 Big Game Awards Measurement Guidelines

Deer & Elk

Moose

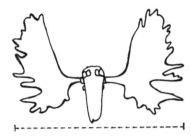

Horns

Caribou

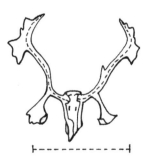

Tusks

Turkey

Point Measurement

Courtesy of the North American Hunting Club

Trophy Hunter's Wild Game Cookbook
Index of Recipe Names and Categories

Index

Index

Index

**Barry Gorden Barbour (left) and Donald Barbour (right) hold up some
of the cutthroat trout caught in the Snake River, Jackson Hole, Wyoming.**

Cookbooks Published by Cookbook Resources, LLC
Bringing Family and Friends to the Table

The Best 1001 Short, Easy Recipes
1001 Slow Cooker Recipes
1001 Short, Easy, Inexpensive Recipes
1001 Fast Easy Recipes
1001 America's Favorite Recipes
Easy Slow Cooker Cookbook
Busy Woman's Slow Cooker Recipes
Busy Woman's Quick & Easy Recipes
365 Easy Soups and Stews
365 Easy Chicken Recipes
365 Easy One-Dish Recipes
365 Easy Soup Recipes
365 Easy Vegetarian Recipes
365 Easy Casserole Recipes
365 Easy Pasta Recipes
365 Easy Slow Cooker Recipes
Super Simple Cupcake Recipes
Leaving Home Cookbook and Survival Guide
Essential 3-4-5 Ingredient Recipes
Ultimate 4 Ingredient Cookbook
Easy Cooking with 5 Ingredients
The Best of Cooking with 3 Ingredients
Easy Diabetic Recipes
Ultimate 4 Ingredient Diabetic Cookbook
4-Ingredient Recipes for 30-Minute Meals
Cooking with Beer
The Washington Cookbook
The Pennsylvania Cookbook
The California Cookbook
Best-Loved New England Recipes
Best-Loved Canadian Recipes
Best-Loved Recipes from the Pacific Northwest

Easy Slow Cooker Recipes (Handbook with Photos)
Cool Smoothies (Handbook with Photos)
Easy Cupcake Recipes (Handbook with Photos)
Easy Soup Recipes (Handbook with Photos)
Classic Tex-Mex and Texas Cooking
Best-Loved Southern Recipes
Classic Southwest Cooking
Miss Sadie's Southern Cooking
Classic Pennsylvania Dutch Cooking
The Quilters' Cookbook
Healthy Cooking with 4 Ingredients
Trophy Hunter's Wild Game Cookbook
Recipe Keeper
Simple Old-Fashioned Baking
Quick Fixes with Cake Mixes
Kitchen Keepsakes & More Kitchen Keepsakes
Cookbook 25 Years
Texas Longhorn Cookbook
Gifts for the Cookie Jar
All New Gifts for the Cookie Jar
The Big Bake Sale Cookbook
Easy One-Dish Meals
Easy Potluck Recipes
Easy Casseroles Cookbook
Easy Desserts
Sunday Night Suppers
Easy Church Suppers
365 Easy Meals
Gourmet Cooking with 5 Ingredients
Muffins In A Jar
A Little Taste of Texas
A Little Taste of Texas II
Ultimate Gifts for the Cookie Jar

**cookbook
resources** LLC
www.cookbookresources.com
Toll-Free 866-229-2665
Your Ultimate Source for Easy Cookbooks

(Left to right) Donald, Judy, Barry Gorden and Barry Barbour stand in front of the Alaskan brown bear killed by Barry Barbour. Read about the hunt and subsequent trip in the story "There's a Bear Coming Down the Freeway" on page 113.